Joseph B Stratton

Extracts from an Elder's Diary

Joseph B Stratton

Extracts from an Elder's Diary

ISBN/EAN: 9783337018627

Printed in Europe, USA, Canada, Australia, Japan

Cover: Foto ©ninafisch / pixelio.de

More available books at **www.hansebooks.com**

EXTRACTS

FROM

AN ELDER'S DIARY

EDITED BY

REV JOSEPH B. STRATTON, D. D.,

NATCHEZ, MISS.

Richmond, Va.:
PRESBYTERIAN COMMITTEE OF PUBLICATION.

NOTE.

The permission to publish the extracts from an elder's diary contained in this volume was given by a competent authority, at the request of the present editor, to whom the privilege of reading the original manuscript had been accorded. The request was made in the hope that a record of the actual labors, trials and experiences of one bearing the important office of ruling elder in the Presbyterian Church, interspersed with illustrative incidents, might be serviceable to this branch of the Christian ministry. Treatises and manuals, proposing to throw light upon the spirit and manner in which the functions of the eldership should be discharged, have been numerous of late. The fact may be indicative of an awakened conviction on the part of the teaching ministry that their work needs to be buttressed by an increased efficiency on the part of these coadjutors taken from the body of a church's members. The house given to the former to build is so "exceedingly magnifical" in its design and proportions that it calls for an expenditure of talent and toil greater than any one man can furnish. It has been thought by the editor that the living picture afforded by these annals of an elder's attempts to do his duty might be a helpful supplement to directories of a more definite kind, and hence they have been given to the public.

It is hardly necessary to add, that in copying these extracts care has been taken to conceal names of persons and places, so as to avoid the risk of trespassing upon the sanctities of private life. But few changes in the language have been required in preparing the manuscript for publication. The facts introduced, I have reason to know, are realities, not fictions; and the selections from the body of the diary have been made with the best judgment the editor could exercise.

J. B. STRATTON.

"*Sunset Lodge,*" *Natchez, Miss.*

CONTENTS.

I.
THE STRUGGLE, ... 7

II.
THE DECISION, ... 11

III.
PREPARATION, ... 17

IV.
A PRACTICAL PROBLEM, ... 20

V.
A VICTORY, ... 25

VI.
NEW CROSSES, ... 32

VII.
PEACEMAKING, ... 37

VIII.
THE PRESBYTERY, ... 44

IX.
AN INQUIRER, ... 50

X.
THE SABBATH-SCHOOL, ... 59

XI.	PAGE.
A Revival,	65
XII.	
A Romance,	72
XIII.	
A Pestilence,	81
XIV.	
The General Assembly,	94
XV.	
Pastoral Changes,	106
XVI.	
Tribulation,	110
XVII.	
Session Meetings,	122
XVIII.	
Sociability.	128
XIX.	
Church Discipline,	135
XX.	
Sovereign Grace,	143
XXI.	
Spiritual Communications,	150
XXII.	
Eventide	162

EXTRACTS

FROM

AN ELDER'S DIARY.

EXTRACT I.

THE STRUGGLE.

May 18, 1865.—To my surprise—I might almost say dismay—I have received notice to-day of my election at a recent meeting of our congregation to the office of ruling elder. The announcement has thrown my mind into a tumult which has almost amounted to an agony. I seem to be standing in the presence of a mountain, with a voice sounding in my ears, bidding me to lift it. At every glance I take at the stupendous object, the larger it seems to grow, and the more my consciousness of my inability to bear its weight overwhelms me. My inclinations prompt me at once to decline the call. My judgment, as far as I can be said to have any in my present confusion of mind, sides with my inclinations. I am averse to positions of prominence or leadership.

My disposition leads me to shrink from responsibility and the criticism to which office exposes one. I have not enjoyed the advantages of literary culture. My training has been largely of a practical sort. I feel myself at home in every-day business matters, but in the higher field of ecclesiastical legislation and spiritual science I am a novice, needing to be taught rather than presuming to teach. Besides, I am painfully lacking in self-confidence. I lose my command of such resources as I may really possess, when called upon to act in the eyes of a multitude. My bewilderment is oppressive! I fear to take a step in any direction, lest it should be a wrong one. Lord, help me! Send me light.

Sunday, May 21.—The last three days have been so absorbed in the consideration of this great question of duty which has been thrust upon me that I have had little capacity for my ordinary employments. My repugnance to accepting the office proposed to me continues, perhaps, as decided as ever; but sometimes the suspicion steals into my mind that there may, to some extent, be a carnal bias affecting my way of looking at the matter; and fearing that I might be unduly swayed by this, I have tried, with the simplicity of a little child, to follow the counsel of the apostle: "If any man lack wisdom, let him ask of God."

I have felt, at the close of this holy day, in which I seem to have been unusually conscious of the nearness of that divine inspirer, that the aspect of the harassing problem has somewhat changed, and that some of the factors in it which at first appalled me have been withdrawn, and others which I had failed to appreciate have come into view.

I think I am indebted, in part, for the comparative composure I enjoy to-night to some thoughts uttered by our pastor in his sermon this morning. Speaking of our Lord's remark to his disciples, in Matthew x. 20, "It is not ye that speak, but the Spirit of your Father which speaketh in you," he explained that "speaking," here, might be understood as including all forms of testimony by which men may bear witness to Christ, or render service in the propagating of his religion; and, while admitting that the immediate reference of the saying was to the supernatural aid his disciples might expect in their controversies with their opponents, he argued that all believers are authorized to expect from their heavenly Father the help of the Holy Spirit in fitting them for duty, more confidently even than children are to expect bread from the hand of a natural parent. (Luke xi. 13.) "As the presence of the Holy Spirit," he continued, "implies the exercise of his power in some way, there is valid ground for the expectation that this power will be exercised in behalf of every sincere Christian who is striving, whether by speech or work, to bring men to the knowledge of the truth as it is in Jesus."

In revolving these thoughts, I find that an estimate of the efficiency I might bring into the office set before me is not to be limited by the paucity of my personal endowments, but that the declaration, "It is not ye that speak, but the Spirit of your Father," carries me out of my feeble self, and shows me a reserve of force lying behind or above me, whose resources are available for me simply upon the asking.

The train of my reflections has been, in some measure, assuring; and I go to my rest repeating the words of Moses (Exodus xxxiii. 15): "If thy presence go not with me, carry us not up hence," but venturing to add, with a hesitating confidence, "If that presence will go with me, Lord, I will lean upon thy strength and go up."

EXTRACT II.

THE DECISION.

Sunday, June 4.—I review the events of this day with peculiar solemnity. It seems as if the vows of consecration, which I made ten years ago when I was admitted to the communion of the church, had been repeated with a special emphasis and a special precision of aim and purpose. If I said then, with an earnest heart, "Lord, what wilt thou have me to do?" I have with tenfold earnestness renewed the appeal to-day.

My assent to the call having been given in the previous week, it was arranged that the ordination should take place this morning, in connection with the administration of the Lord's supper, for which this was the regular season. It was a happy conjunction. It was a good position, in the presence of the symbols of the Saviour's service for his people, for an honest disciple to get a view of the measure of service due to him. It was impossible not to respond to the import of the sacred festival in the terms of the apostle's confession, "To me to live is Christ."

The opportunity was a good one, too, in which to realize that my investiture with office was a fact as well as a form; for it gave me the privilege, as a minister in the Lord's house, of presenting to my fellow-believers the emblematic bread and cup, which, by his own ordinance, were to attest the redemption wrought through his death till he should come again.

While the series of thoughts or convictions by which the result just consummated has been reached is fresh in my mind, I wish to record them deliberately, thinking that a recollection of them may be useful to me in coming time.

First, then, I cannot entertain a doubt that the congregating of Christians in the form of a church, as practiced by the apostles, included in it the appointing of a certain class of persons to be teachers and rulers in each particular body. The economy, or *house-law* of the new family, called necessarily for such a class. Accordingly, when a band of disciples had been gathered together, in several cities in Asia Minor, by Paul and Barnabas (Acts xiv. 23), and a permanent organization had to be introduced, under which their corporate life might be protected and cultivated, they, that is, Paul, an inspired ambassador of Christ, and Barnabas, his chosen associate, "ordained them" elders (or presbyters) in every city; and, then, "having prayed with fasting and commended them to the Lord on whom they believed," left them under the sole charge of these officers. Similarly, I find that the apostle commissioned Titus his deputy to "ordain elders in every city" in Crete. (Titus i. 5.) Uniformly, I may say, wherever I see a church referred to in apostolic writings, I see the "elders" conjoined with it as a constituent and representative element. (See Acts xi. 30; xx. 17; Jas. v. 14; 1 Pet. v. 1.) I am sure, therefore, that the office that I have consented to accept has the authentic warrant of an institution of the head of the church.

Second, It is clear to me, from the tenor of the Scripture allusions and the probabilities of the case, that there was, ordinarily at least, a plurality of these elders in each church; and, if so, "diversities of gifts," which led to a diversity of function, such as now distinguishes the "teaching" from the "ruling" elder in the Presbyterian Church. I am satisfied, therefore, that the office with which I have been invested has a place in the divine plan, and needs to be filled, in order to perfect the organization of a church. It strikes me that this multiplied way of exercising the oversight of the flock is eminently the result of the wisdom of the Holy Ghost.

Third, I am constrained to conclude that, owing to the incompetency caused by the old age or confirmed ill-health of some of the members of the eldership in this church, there is, at this time, a patent necessity for an addition to their number. It is clearly the duty of *some* individual or individuals in the male constituency of the church, in this exigency, to lend their services, however diffident they may be as to their worthiness, to this branch of the Lord's work. The appeal addresses itself to me, as well as to others. It is enforced by the voice of my brethren. If it is I whom the Master needs, I must not refuse to obey.

Fourth, I see that many who, like Moses and Jeremiah, have had a clear vocation from God to do service in his kingdom, and have shrunk from the mission assigned them through conscious unfitness, have, nevertheless, when obediently taking up their burden, "out of weakness been made strong"; and by their history I am admonished to be distrustful of those self-distrusting scruples which led me, at first view, to object to a proposed work for God.

Fifth, I find a growing attractiveness in the work I am invited to take up, from the conviction that it will not only add to my opportunities for doing good, but will contribute largely to my growth in personal piety. I am sure the "one thing" I have set before me as the supreme end of my present life is, "to press toward the mark for the prize of the high calling of God in Christ Jesus." I persuade myself that in obeying this call of the church I shall realize more sensibly the force of this "high calling." I shall be brought into more conscious sympathy and fellowship with Christ. In "losing" my life for his sake, in giving my thoughts and cares to the interests of his cause. I may hope to experience the blessed result of "saving" it, in the sense of quickening and maturing the spiritual principle within me. I may find myself growing richer in grace in proportion as I abridge my schemes of self-seeking (which is the name for worldly business), and consecrate my energies to the advancement of Christ's kingdom. There is an inspiration in this idea which gives me courage, and which I cannot but think comes from above. The peace it has brought me is peculiar. May I not regard it as the "perfect peace" promised to those "whose minds are stayed on God"?

Sixth, I have been confirmed in the conclusion to which I have come, by an exalted view of the nature of that faith which I am exercising. It appears to me it is a sort of transmutation—a putting of him in whom I trust in the place of myself, or a transfer of my poor personality to that of my Chief, who has said to his messenger, "Go, and I will be with thee!" The work I am to do must be done by a human instrument, by human methods; but the Being who has allowed me to link myself with him can give a potency to my efforts beyond what they inherently possess. I will measure my possible efficiency by that which I know belongs to the Master with whom I am identified. This seems to be the view of faith which St. Paul expresses when he says (Gal. ii. 20), "I live, yet not I, but Christ liveth in me"; and (Phil. iv. 13) "I can do all things through Christ which strengtheneth me." Here, too, in the confidence that in the sincere endeavor to do the work proposed to me I shall be acting under an inspiration and an invigoration derived from fellowship with Christ, I find a ground of comfort as I contemplate the grave responsibilities I am about to assume. "We have this treasure in earthen vessels, that the excellency of the power may be of God, and not of us." (2 Cor. iv. 7.)

EXTRACT III.

PREPARATION.

Sunday, July 2.—I have been occupied during the past month in studying, as I have had opportunity, the nature of the office of ruling elder, and the form of practical work which it includes. For this purpose I have gone, first, to the apostolic writings, and sought to get from this source a definite idea of what the infallible founders of the Christian church intended that the presbyters whom they ordained should be and do. This idea, I think, is carefully and correctly reproduced in the section touching the ruling elder in Chapter IV. of the Form of Government of our church. In addition, I have consulted such of the published treatises and hand-books upon the subject as were within my reach. The effect has been a helpful one. I feel that I have a precise and intelligent conception, at least as to the main points, of what is required of me by conscience and the body which has called me to be its overseer; and my hope is that I shall be able, in my manner of executing my office, to bear with me a fixed consciousness of its obligations, and not leave them to be suggested by casual impulses or merely ceremonial demands. Always, and everywhere, I want to remember my ministry and to "make full proof of it."

It has seemed to me, knowing as I do, and as everybody does, what is expected of the pastor of a church, and recognizing the ruling elder as a connecting link between him and his flock, touching both parties in his relations and functions, that the duty of the elder may be comprehended in this one statement—that he is to endeavor in all things except those which belong specially to the pastoral office to make the pastor's work his own. Through his labors the pastor's efficiency is to be ramified. He is to be the arm which moves in accord with the will of the head. What the pastor preaches in the way of doctrine and precept he is to reproduce as a "living epistle," which may be read of all men, in his character and deportment; and what the pastor enjoins as a Christian duty he is to endorse by his consistent example. He is to be the reflector by which the force of the pulpit is to be conveyed to the people; and the reporter by whom the needs of the people are to be disclosed to the pastor. St. Paul seems to have regarded Timothy as standing somewhat in this relation to himself, when he wrote to the Corinthians (1 Cor. iv. 17): "For this cause have I sent unto you Timotheus, who is my beloved son, and faithful in the Lord, who shall *bring you into remembrance of my ways* which be in Christ, *as I teach* everywhere in every church."

I intend to keep this general idea in my mind as a convenient summary of particular duties. I fancy that it will give a play and scope to the sensibilities in my work, which, perhaps, a mere attention to a routine or a schedule might fail to supply. I fully appreciate the necessity for order as a condition of success in any undertaking, and I will try to observe it; but my disposition leads to chafe under the strict application of lines and angles in religious services. With the regularity of Ezekiel's wheel, I like to see the free motion of the "Spirit" which is in it.

EXTRACT IV.

A PRACTICAL PROBLEM.

Sunday, July 23.—As happens in most cases with those who bear the office of ruling elder, I am embarrassed by the absorbing demands of secular avocations. My time, for the greater part of each week-day, belongs to my employers. I am religiously bound to show myself a just steward. I have a wife and three children, whom, by careful management, I can support comfortably on my salary. My solicitude for them naturally reaches beyond the present moment, and calls for forethought and scheming in order to protect them against the possible needs of the future. The obligation to provide for those of one's own house, which St. Paul so forcibly urges, is one which I keenly and constantly feel. How to make this consistent with the business of my Father's house is the problem with which I am confronted. I must exercise the same patient deliberation in this matter that I am accustomed to use in adjusting the apparently conflicting accounts which baffle me in my book-keeping. Fidelity to God and fidelity to man are both right, and, when properly conceived and defined, cannot be at variance with each other. A few points, at least, seem to me clear now.

First, I take it that for all that I am really required to do in the way of spiritual work there must be, somewhere, an opportunity. If, after proper inquiry and experiment, none can be found for any particular act or service, I may make myself easy in the conclusion that *that* is not required of me.

Second, Through the beneficent arrangement of the divine law, I have secured to me one-seventh of my time, through the recurrence of the weekly Sabbath. A judicious use of this season may be made to yield an abundant opportunity for Christian labor, without diverting it from its appointed end as a season of sacred resting. The Sabbath, in enjoining rest, does not proscribe activity. It recognizes the fact that rest is not sluggishness, but the sensation of relief which one feels in passing from one wholesome form of activity to another. The mere shifting from the mind the burden of weekly cares and responsibilities brings with it a sensible infusion of freedom and exhilaration to a jaded spirit. The hours devoted to public and private worship are eminently restful in their influence. The atmosphere of home-life is a delightful substitute for the bustle and strife of the market and the factory. And then the portion of the day which may be given to out-door labor of a religious sort, by its throwing the energy of mind and body into new and interesting channels, may be made to minister refreshment through what appears to be toil. My Sabbaths, I am determined, shall be harvest days. I see golden fruitage in them.

And, third, I will "gather up the fragments," husband the odd moments of my time. I will pluck ears of grain as I plod on my daily errands through the cornfields. A little incident which befell me yesterday, trifling as the shaking of a leaf on a mulberry tree, has taught me that by vigilance and celerity an occasion may be found for thrusting a good deed into those interstices of time which are usually so minute as to be deemed incapable of being turned to any useful account.

As I was leisurely returning from my dinner, I met on —— street a little girl whom I knew as a Sunday-school scholar. I stopped to take her by the hand and ask after her family, when, with the eagerness to tell news which is characteristic of children, she said: "Mrs. S——, in there," pointing to an adjoining house, "is very sick." Mrs. S—— was known to me as a worthy widow woman who depended upon her labor for the support of herself and two young children. I looked at my watch, and found that I had ten minutes to spare before I was due at my office. I knocked at the door, and, in answer to a feeble response, went in. A moment's glance and a few inquiries were enough to satisfy me that the poor woman was, indeed, very sick, and that her needs were numerous and urgent. I cheered her with a few comforting words, and promised to send some one to her relief. I hastened on my way, and fortunately meeting a good lady, who, I knew, was a member of one of our church associations, I reported the case to her, and arranged for the immediate supply of all the sufferer's wants. To-day, on my way to church, I called and found a nurse at her bedside, a physician in attendance, and an ample stock of provisions in the house. I thought to myself, that little blank of ten minutes was well filled up; and the sweepings of a man's time, as well as those of the United States' mint, may be found to contain particles of gold.

With the exercise of watchfulness in detecting opportunities, and promptness in using them, I am convinced many forms of Christian work can be inserted into the stern routine of the busiest life. The eagerness with which these cabmen, whom I see daily on the streets, keep their eyes glancing from side to side, in order to pick up a passenger, has often suggested to me the reflection that, if we laborers for God were half as zealous in our endeavors to attract souls into his kingdom, we should be able more frequently at the day's end to make report to our Master of palpable proofs of our fidelity in our calling.

O Lord, help me to be as careful in my service of thee as I am in my efforts to fulfil my obligations to my earthly employer!

EXTRACT V.

A VICTORY.

August 16.—I feel to-night like making a special record of my gratitude to God for the aid he has given me in the performance of a duty which, at first, was contemplated by me with serious misgivings. I refer to the matter of prayer in public. I cannot but regard the degree to which I have overcome my reluctance to engage in this exercise, and the command of thoughts and words which I have acquired in leading in it, as a gracious answer to my supplications for divine aid in the discharge of my office in this particular. It seems to me, as I reflect upon it, that this gift, if I may humbly call it such, means more than a single endowment. It indicates a broadening and an elevation of the whole sphere of my spiritual being. If it be fact as well as poetry, that "prayer is the Christian's vital breath," it is not an unreasonable inference that an aptitude for prayer is significant of an enlargement of the entire religious life. As I analyze my experience, it appears to me that prayer is intimately associated with every stage of its progress. St. James puts (chapter iv. 8) the two propositions, "Draw nigh to God, and he will draw nigh to you," in as close a conjunction as that of the two hemispheres of a globe.

After a long period of aberration from God, through indifference, worldliness of mind, and devotion to carnal gratification, I was led to notice the fact that if God were a being co-existent with me in the world, my course of life had been a perpetual abandonment of him. The thought startled me. It led to a study of the claims of God to my faith, and to a conviction that he, and the religion which acknowledged him, were tremendous realities. In a dim sort of way, as of one seeing him afar off, I had drawn nigh to God. It was a trembling first step. I must get nearer; but in my conscious guilt I did not dare to approach him. I felt my need of a healer of the breach—a medium of access; and I found this revealed to me in the mission and work of our Lord Jesus Christ. I then discovered a ground upon which I could *pray;* and I did pray, and the prayer, based upon Christ's mediation, brought me light, and peace, and assurance that God had pardoned and accepted me; and thus I "drew nigh" to God, and he "drew nigh" to me, in a reconciliation like that which united the prodigal and his father. And I have found ever since, that my "fellowship with the Father and the Son" has been concurrent with the genuineness of my prayers.

I began my religious life thus, I may say, with the impression that prayer was something more than the begging of favors; that it was a mode of communing with God—a process in which there was a mutual drawing nigh between him and my soul. This impression, in proportion as it was kept in operation, made prayer a very serious and solemn exercise. It overshadowed my spirit very sensibly with the one great idea of the presence of God. It had another effect: it produced what I might call an abiding prayerful frame, out of which grew a habit of mingling communing with God with the continuous workings of my mind in its secret recesses. It was a living, if I may so express it, in constant touch of God, so that prayer became an element in all breathing and acting, although no outward sign revealed it. This informal way of communing with God did not abate, but I think rather increased the relish with which I engaged in the more deliberate devotions of the closet; and, I may add, gave me an aptness in throwing my own mind into the currents of public prayer, as offered by others.

These reflections upon my early religious

life, suffused as they are with the recollection of the warmth of a "first love," recall to me sadly that I was derelict in one important particular, that of family worship. It was some years after our marriage that my wife and I connected ourselves with the church; and during that period it had not occurred to us that we ought to sanctify our home-life by such a practice. At our reception into the church the duty was enjoined upon us by our pastor, and for a time was observed by us. It was hard, however, under the pressure of business engagements and the cares of the household, to keep up the practice with regularity, and ultimately it was suspended. It has been resumed now, never to be intermitted again.

The high conception I have entertained of the augustness of prayer as communion with God has, I think, affected me with a dread of allowing a regard for the mere fitness of style and structure to impair the devotional element in the offering of public prayer. Hence, until recently, I have persuaded myself that my objections were good, and have declined to participate in the prayers at our weekly meetings. In the nighness of my human hearers I foresaw, as I thought, a barrier to that nighness between God and myself that I felt was necessary in prayer.

After my induction into my office as elder, I recognized that scruple, in this particular, was standing in the way of an obvious duty. I looked into my heart carefully, faced the question conscientiously, and soon was cheered by the conviction that private inclination had gone over, largely, to the side of duty. I could say, "Not as I will, but as thou willest." The only point which embarrassed me now was the practical one, Am I able to do that which I am willing to do?

The answer to this doubt came in the thought—the grace which has wrought in me "to will" can just as easily work in me "to do." My next step was to bring my deficiency into contact with the sufficiency which I knew to be in God. I prayed alone that he would give me the ability to pray before my fellowmen. I told him my infirmity, and besought the aid which should lift me above the gravitation of a morbid self-consciousness and a distracting environment. I drew very nigh to him and asked him not to let me lose the sense of my nighness to him when I should attempt to open my lips in the presence of a congregation. This step brought additional strength.

My next one was to reflect that the operations of grace imply and include a corresponding effort on the part of the subject of them to gain the blessing which he desires to have given him. While "the preparation of the heart in man is from the Lord," the bestowing of it pre-supposes that the man who seeks it has sought, to the best of his ability, to prepare his heart for it. I seconded my appeals to God, therefore, by striving to fix in my mind a definite idea of what the purpose in a public prayer should be, and what should properly be the form of it. I said, it ought to voice, as far as possible, the mind of the company in whose stead and behalf it is uttered. It need not, and generally ought not to, be long. It ought not to be elaborate, or ambitious, or eccentric. It ought not to aim at comprehending everything. It ought to be regulated and modified by the controlling thought, "I am speaking to God." I did not attempt to compose prayers, but I did endeavor to familiarize my mind with the material which ordinarily pertained to prayer, and, to some extent, with the terms and phrases which were suited to it. For this purpose I studied carefully such published forms of prayer as commended themselves to my judgment; and especially sought to gain some command of the inimitable vocabulary of devotion contained in the Holy Scriptures.

A VICTORY. 31

Having previously given my consent, I was spared the shock which might have been the effect of an unexpected summons, when I was first called upon to lead in prayer at our weekly service; and was gratified to find that with considerable composure I was able to keep my mind intent upon the few topics which succeeded one another in my brief effusion. I had done my duty; and I felt happier, especially when, at the close of the meeting, a brother took me by the hand and said, quietly, "Thank you for that prayer!"

Since then I have come to realize that facility in this exercise is itself an answer to prayer—a thought which is adapted to give confidence to the possessor of it, and at the same time make him humble in the use of it. I am satisfied, too, that this is a gift to be coveted as a means of communicating good to others. A fit and seasonable prayer often becomes the vehicle by which some one's benumbed and crippled soul is lifted out of its confusion, and enabled to feel that its latent yearnings have been made clear, and its dumb desires have become articulate, through the sympathetic words of another.

God help me to appreciate the talent, in the limited measure in which I have received it, more and more, and to be ready to use it for his glory as opportunity is offered to me!

EXTRACT VI.

NEW CROSSES.

Sunday, October 1.—The past summer has seen me pressing on in official experience and acquaintance with the trials of presbyterial service. During the absence of Dr. N———, our pastor, on his vacation, I have been required, on several occasions, to conduct the weekly prayer-meeting. My first effort in this line was attended by a perturbation of spirit which, I am sure, if I had begun to cherish any feeling of self-sufficiency, would have taken it all out of me. Nothing but the voice of conscience reminding me that, as I had put my hand to the plough, I could not consistently look back, nerved me to undertake the formidable task.

Remembering a rule which I had adopted in my secular operations, that in order to the doing of anything I must first get a clear conception of the thing I had to do, I set before me, as distinctly as I could, the object for which our meeting was to be held. I then endeavored to arrange the series of exercises so that each should have a bearing upon this object. The address, or lecture, was the part of the service which most appalled me, for I was neither "a scribe learned in the law," nor a ready speaker. However, by keeping in mind that a simple man must attempt only simple things, and by looking to the Giver of wisdom for help, I braced myself to the work. My wife, as we reached the lecture-room, added her counsel: "My dear, now do be short."

After announcing one stirring hymn, I proposed another, and the singing put the audience into a good frame of mind. A brother who was accustomed to lead followed with a fervent prayer. Another song and prayer kept up the flame of interest, and by the time the Scripture selections were to be read my hearers were far more in the humor of devotion than of criticism. I read from Luke, chapter xix., the account of our Lord's visit to Zaccheus at his house, and added several other passages from the Old and New Testaments, in which God appears as making special revelations of his favor towards pious households. Without any formal introduction, and without an allusion to myself as a novice in the art of exposition, I stated my subject, "The Presence of Christ in the Home," and in my brief unfolding of it I made three points: *First*, The ultimate purpose of the family institution, the furnishing of subjects for the kingdom of God; *Second*, The facilities afforded by it for this end, in the varied motives, means, and opportunities for moulding character included in it; and *Third*, The promises which assured us that Christ was always ready to bring the efficiency of his gracious presence to bless our efforts where the doors of our homes were not closed against him. I had but little to say in the amplification of these points, beyond sustaining them by testimony drawn from Scripture, and closed my remarks by the simple question, "Brethren, is the kind of life which our children, our friends, our servants, are witnessing in our homes such as would give them the impression that Jesus is abiding there from day to day?" With a prayer and a hymn breathing the desire that there might be more homes amongst us in which the Saviour was always, as in the house in Bethany, finding an open door and a loving welcome, the service closed, and I went home with little self-praise, but much praise to God, in my heart. My subsequent efforts, though never free from some embarrassment, were, of course, less embarrassing.

A sorer trial, however, awaited me when, on last Saturday, a note was received from the senior elder, saying that as the supply expected

NEW CROSSES.

to fill our pulpit on the Sabbath had failed us, and he was confined at home by sickness, he particularly requested that I should conduct the worship at the church on the following day. I was staggered at the thought of occupying a position of such prominence, and was disposed at once to pronounce the thing impossible. Something kept me from putting this response in writing. Something whispered to my conscience that I had promised to go work in any part of the Lord's vineyard in which I might be needed. Something reminded me that my infirmities had been graciously helped thus far in every case where I had undertaken a difficult duty. Little by little, at these suggestions, my reluctance gave way, and my purpose was formed. The time was short, the urgency of the case gave intensity to my mental operations, and in a brief space the whole order of services was mapped out. Spurgeon, abbreviated, furnished me with a sermon, and the aid of a brother elder was secured for the devotional exercises. As I look back to-night over the accomplished task, I feel like drawing a long breath, as one who has crossed a perilous chasm on a frail bridge; and a passage which I read this morning from the thirty-fourth Psalm, verses 4 and 5, occurs to me as a fit expression of my present emotions. The good monitor at my side, in her discreet way, has just remarked, "I trembled all over when I saw you go into that pulpit. But I believe I would be willing to see you go there again!"

EXTRACT VII.

PEACEMAKING.

December 1.—The crookedness which inheres in human nature, even after it has been straightened by divine grace, I suppose, will reveal itself in some form and in certain cases in every body of Christians. The Saviour's prayers, "Forgive us our trespasses," and "Lead us not into temptation," seem to imply that we are never to assume that we are exempt from its operation. It is a vicious element left clinging to our moral system, perhaps, to guard us against the dangerous fancy that we are already perfect; or it may be intended to serve as the resisting power, by conflict with which our spiritual strength needs to be maintained and developed.

I have to make confession that I myself, who ought to be "an ensample to the flock," was recently betrayed into an exhibition of this perverse principle, by which I have been deeply humbled, although, I hope, ultimately benefited. The apparently negligent misplacing of some important mail-matter by a clerk at the post-office had given me serious trouble, and led me, perhaps too sharply, to charge him with his fault. He resented my reproof in a tone so offensive that I repeated my charge in plainer and more emphatic terms. This exasperated him still more, and drew from him an abusive denunciation of the church officers for some ill-treatment of his wife, who was a member of the church, in the matter of her "sitting." This allegation I knew to be utterly groundless, and pronounced it so, and turned from him, angry myself, and leaving him in a tempest of passion. I chafed under the irritation produced by this altercation, until gradually, as the fever subsided, I awoke to a calm view of the unseemly temper I had exhibited. I was shocked at the attitude in which I had allowed myself to be placed. I let the day pass, that both parties might regain sobriety; and the next morning addressed a note to my antagonist, in which, without an allusion to his part in the affair, I deplored my own as hasty and unbecoming my character as a Christian; retracted all objectionable language that I had used, and expressed the hope that our former friendly relations might not be interrupted by my intemperate conduct. In a few hours a reply came, frank in its tone and pronouncing the unpleasantness as at an end. Our intercourse has been cordial ever since, but I have learned a lesson as to the duty of circumspectness.

What I was thinking about, however, when this incident came into my mind, was an effort at peacemaking between two disaffected members of our church, in which I was engaged early this week. It was a case of discord between husband and wife. They were plain people, but respectable for their decent and regular lives. The woman had ceased for some time to attend worship, and upon the fact being mentioned on some occasion by our pastor to the husband, he had revealed to him that a "root of bitterness" had sprung up in their home in the shape of dissension, and that his wife, in consequence, had carried her "contrariness," as he called it, to the point of refusing fellowship with him in going to the house of God. "I don't know what to do with her," was the poor man's lament. "She will not let me talk to her. I wish you would come and set us to rights." A time was fixed upon for a visit, and Dr. N——, not a little to my alarm, summoned me to go with him, "as a silent partner," I remarked, in consenting.

Our greeting of the pair when they made their appearance was specially cordial, and a little time was given to the usual commonplaces of courtesy. At length Dr. N———, in the kindest of tones, remarked: "You have not been well, Mrs. A———. I have missed you from several of our last meetings."

"Well—yes—not sick exactly," she replied, in a hesitating way, "but———," then stopped.

"It has not been trouble of mind, I hope?" inquired the doctor.

"Yes, sir," she replied, in a passionate explosion, "yes, sir, and worse than that; it has been trouble of heart."

"My dear madam, you distress me deeply," said the doctor. "What is the matter?"

"Ask *him!* ask *him!*" was her reply, pointing to her husband.

The doctor's eye turned to the latter, who, with a good deal of emotion in his voice, stammered out: "Dr. N———, you are our pastor, and have always been our friend. I will tell you the truth, and I beg you to help us if you can. I don't want to speak against Susan. She has been a good wife to me, and maybe I have done wrong by her. We disagreed about the bringing-up of our daughter. She is just fifteen years old, you know, and is her mother's pride. She has let her stop school, and go to parties, and drive out with young men—and—

and——" and here he, too, broke down. In a moment he added: "It is jealousy for the girl. She says I love the boy best; but God knows I love them both, and their mother, too, as I love my own soul!"

The scene was becoming affecting. I ventured to interpose, in a cheerful way, "Why, this is only the old story of what occurs, I suspect, in nearly all families. Wife and I have more discussions over the management of our children than over anything else; but we know that we both love them and desire their good, and, when we differ, we talk kindly over our respective methods, and pray over them, too, and soon come to an agreement. Perhaps you and Mrs. A—— have not prayed enough over this matter."

"I could not pray," sobbed the woman, "I was so hurt!"

"I propose that Dr. N—— pray now," I said, and, by a common impulse, we all fell on our knees, and the doctor did pray, and prayed with a heart in fullest sympathy with the distressed couple, and, it seemed to me, in very unison with the pity felt for them by a sympathizing Saviour.

When we rose, the doctor, in a clear, quiet way, said, "I see it all now. You both love this dear child, and your love has made you, in the one case, too indulgent, and in the other, perhaps, too strict. You both desire her welfare. Let me tell you that you cannot do her a worse wrong than to let discord enter your home. The Spirit of God flies from the abodes of strife. It seems to me, madam, that your husband is right in wishing Annie to remain a school-girl for at least another year, and to familiarize herself with household avocations; and you, perhaps, have been too impatient under opposition to your views. Think it all over, and I am sure you will see that I am right."

Tears were running down the man's cheeks, and the woman, with a bowed head, murmured, as if to herself, "I have been very wicked—very wicked!"

"Where is Annie? Cannot I see her?" asked the doctor; and it was a relief when the mother left us to call her.

The doctor took the girl gently by the hand, upon her entering, and said: "My child, I baptized you when your parents gave you to the Lord. Promise me that you will obey them, and do all that you can for their comfort."

She replied, "I will," and then the doctor added: "Now, I want to see you all at our prayer-meeting to-morrow night; and, besides, I have a special invitation to you all from Mrs. N—— that you will be present at a little reception we are to have at the manse on next Tuesday evening, the twentieth anniversary of our marriage."

There was a perceptible brightness in the aspect of the group as we left them; and my companion ejaculated, as we reached the street, "God make our words as the precious ointment of Aaron!"

EXTRACT VIII.

THE PRESBYTERY.

April 10, 1866.—I returned last night from a five days' absence, in attendance upon the spring meeting of presbytery, as the representative of our church. It cost me considerable effort, and some inconvenience, to leave home and business, but the desire of the session that I should go was so urgent, and was so enforced by the consideration that my refusal would bring upon the church the reproach of having to report "no elder present," that I stifled all objections and made my arrangements to go. I am thankful now that I did go.

The anticipation of the mission at once brought to my consciousness the fact that I was woefully deficient in my knowledge of church order and parliamentary law. I set to work diligently to inform myself on these subjects. I conferred, also, with our pastor in regard to the business, ordinary and special, which might be expected to claim the attention of presbytery. So, trained and drilled, I made my appearance in time for the opening service, at W———, a neat little railroad town, where some capitalists had established a cotton factory, which gave employment to a large portion of the inhabitants.

My feeling of strangeness soon wore off before the cordial reception accorded me from every quarter. Not unfrequently I was addressed by the term "brother." The initial services were impressive, and the sermon by the venerable Mr. B———, the last moderator, from John xv. 8, tracing the duty of fruitfulness on the part of believers to the love bestowed upon them in the work of him who could call God his "Father," and the grace conferred upon them in permitting and enabling them to "glorify" this Father, was a forcible appeal for consecration to all the followers of the Lord Jesus Christ.

In constituting the presbytery, to my dismay I heard my name nominated for the office of Temporary Clerk. The nomination, I observed, came from one of the junior members of the body. My good patron, Dr. N———, catching my look of embarrassment, rose and stated that he feared this custom of thrusting an office, of which they knew nothing, upon new recruits had in it more of the mischief-loving humor of the college boys' custom of "hazing" than of the regard for expediency and decorum which should characterize an ecclesiastical court, and moved that I should be excused, and somebody else, whom he named, be put in my place. The proposition was carried. In the appointment of committees, I found I was assigned to several places; and I was glad, in this capacity, to render some service in the prosecution of the business of the body. The impressions I have brought away from this first attendance upon a church congress of this kind have been altogether pleasant.

First, It was pleasant to find myself, for a series of days, in a purely religious atmosphere, from which the gross disturbances of worldly pursuits and competitions were banished, and where good-will and Christian love beamed in every face and spake in every utterance.

Second, The half-hour morning prayer-meetings were refreshing seasons, in which a heavenly dew, which proved to be manna, fell upon the opening of each day; and the sermons at night seemed to grow better as they succeeded one another, perhaps from the quickened appetite of those who came to hear them. The sacramental service on the Sabbath morning, with a Sunday-school meeting in the afternoon, and an eloquent sermon at night, made this last day of the feast a golden one.

Third, I was struck with the good humor—I might call it, in some instances, hilarity—which characterized the intercourse of the clerical part of our body. The cordiality of their greetings, and the ringing laughter which often attended their colloquies, convinced me that the phrase "sour-faced Presbyterians" was a slander, growing, most probably, out of the *sour-mindedness* of the critics who used it.

Fourth, I gained an immense amount of information in regard to the methods and results of the working of our church, and an enlarged conviction, I trust, of the duty of Christians devoting more thought, prayer, and money to the support of evangelical enterprises. The work done is a success, like one of those clearings which I often met with on my journey to W——, showing cultivated gaps in the forest, but revealing, each one, the immense stretches of timber land yet to be subdued.

Fifth, One of the pleasantest recollections that I retain is that of my intercourse with the hospitable family among whom I found my home. The household consisted of Mrs. H——, a lady of commanding person, from which all uncomfortable stateliness was removed, and with a sweet aspect, in which dignity was softened by kindness; her three daughters, two of whom were grown, while the third was a merry school-girl, and two sons, both holding positions in the cotton mills. All were professed Christians except the younger son and "Babe," as they still called the youngest girl. They were staunch Presbyterians, and knew why they were so; and were zealous and intelligent supporters of the church, who, through their familiarity with the religious papers and periodicals, kept themselves abreast with its movements. I regard it as a special blessing to have been associated with such a family, and to have witnessed, as I am sure I have done, the power of religion to add a charm distinctively its own to natural beauty and to cultivated grace.

Sixth, One thing more I must not overlook. My fellow-lodger at Mrs. H———'s was the Rev. Mr. McW———, a young minister, who is laboring in a frontier district of our presbytery. Frequent conversations with him have stirred my heart with new emotions of admiration for, and sympathy with, the noble and self-denying work of these home missionaries. That young evangelist has been to me almost a new revelation of the spirit of Christianity. He has convinced me that apostolic zeal and heroism are not dead. If ever I fail in time to come to speak a word in defence of the class to which he belongs, or to give of my substance for their support, "let my tongue cleave to the roof of my mouth, and my right hand forget her cunning."

EXTRACT IX.

AN INQUIRER.

Sunday, September 2.—To-day I have had to undertake a duty of a kind so serious and delicate that I have always shrunk from it. It is that of guiding a soul to Christ. To speak, in general terms, of the claims of Christ to the confidence and love of men; to explain, generally, the way of salvation through faith in his name, or to urge men, generally, to embrace this salvation, has not seemed difficult, nor have I hesitated to attempt it, in my poor way, as the opportunity has been given me. But to sit alone with an anxious inquirer, to see him struggling with a distress which, perhaps, he is unable to explain, and groping after a deliverance which he cannot discover; to unravel the complexity of his spiritual condition, and apply the balm which is needed for his heart's sore—this has seemed to me an exercise of tact and wisdom of which I was incapable. I have been disposed—as, I suppose, most private Christians are when such cases are brought to their notice—to say, "Let us go talk with the minister." In the appeal which was made to me today I could not do this.

I had hardly got seated in my library, after returning from the morning's service, when S. W———, a young man whom I knew very well, was shown into the room, and addressed me abruptly: "Mr. B———, I want to talk with you; I want you to pray for me!"

His look and voice betrayed some deep emotion, and his language, of course, let me see that it was of a religious nature. I took him by the hand, and said to him, "My dear S———, sit down; be composed, and let us talk a while. What is it that is so troubling you?"

"Oh!" he said, "that sermon this morning! It seemed to show me that I have been all wrong when I thought that I was all right. What am I to do with Jesus which is called Christ? What have I been doing with him? I feel more than ever that I need religion, and yet there is something here in religion which I have not understood. What am I to do with Jesus? And what has Jesus to do with me?"

The text had been Pilate's inquiry, in Matthew xxvii. 22.

"This is not a sudden feeling with you? You have been convinced of your need of religion before?" I said, inquiringly.

"Oh! yes," he replied. "You know how religiously I was brought up. The impressions of my early years have never been lost. The example of my father and mother, too, always kept me from questioning the reality and value of religion when sceptical suggestions occurred to me, or were made to me by others. When a boy, I tried to be, and was, I suppose, as the term goes, a 'good boy.' When I grew up, and went into business, I carried with me a tender conscience, for which I have often been ridiculed, and I kept constantly in mind the distinction between right and wrong. I was determined that my employers should find no fault with me, and they never have done so. When I went into society, of which I have been very fond, I did not abandon my religious habits, as I regarded them; but found that my desire to please my companions and my aversion to appearing singular led me often into compliance with practices which I could not justify to myself when the excitement was over. I have a thousand times said to myself, this plan upon which I am living, if there is any religion in it, is giving me neither strength nor comfort. This conviction has troubled me fearfully of late, and it was in my mind when I went to church this morning. As Dr. N——

proceeded with his sermon and made some of his sharp applications, the thought occurred to me, almost like a flash, may not this be the difficulty with me? I have not done what I ought to have done with Jesus. Passages from the Bible about Jesus, which I had been reading all my life without any distinct impression of their meaning, now came crowding upon me with a clearness and a force which they had never had before. The way that I had been treading seemed to become all dark; the way that I needed to take seemed all dark, too; and in my bewilderment I have come to you, for I have confidence in your religion, to ask you to instruct and advise me."

He paused, and looked at me with an exhausted expression, for he had said much more than I can recall. His heart was full, and he had poured it out with a remarkable degree of coherency and fluency. I thought of the story of the young man in Matthew xix. 16-23, and quietly read it to him. "Don't you see," I added, "that this young man was taking no account of sin, as an obstacle in the way of eternal life, in his idea of religion? He would earn eternal life by the doing of good things. His disquietude of mind was due, not to any doubt as to the reality of his obedience as a means of gaining it, but to a fear that the *measure of that obedience might be defective.* 'What lack I yet?' he asks, 'what good more ought I to do?' The Saviour teaches him that obedience, to be genuine, must admit no gradations of less or more. It must be a total conformity to the law of God—such as would make a rich man willing to sell all that he possessed and give the proceeds to the poor, if such a command were laid upon him. A religion based upon obedience must show an obedience which is entire. It must spring from the heart of a man and pervade his whole inner and outer life. It must have in it no weakness of will, no inconstancy of action or affection. Oh! my friend, what mortal man can abide such a test? The young man could not, and you and I cannot. Our obedience is rotten at the very base, and our deviations and omissions, on one side or another, are perpetually revealing our weakness and disturbing our peace. All such deviations and omissions are departures from righteousness, or evidences of a sinful nature expressing itself in sinful acts. Now, here is where 'Jesus which is called Christ' has something, or rather everything, to do for us and with us. Read your New Testament and you will see that his whole work is for sinners and with sinners. Hear St. Paul proclaiming his view of the gospel, 'This is a faithful saying and worthy of all acceptation, that Christ Jesus came into the world to save sinners.' Do you not see a meaning in this passage, and in a hundred others like it, which, perhaps, has never been disclosed to you before? Where your efforts at obedience to the law of God have left you Jesus finds you; that is, in the position of a sinner, and he offers to put you in the position which you have been vainly seeking by your previous effort, that is, that of a righteous man in the sight of God. To this end he says, 'believe in me, trust in me, come to me. Put my work in the place of your old self and its work, and find the ground of your salvation in me and my work as you once did in your supposed obedience.'"

Here my hearer, who had been listening with rapt attention while I had talked, broke in with the remark, "This faith perplexes me! I surely believe in Christ. I have always done so. I have tried to get my ideas of religion from him as an infallible teacher."

"You have believed in him as a teacher," I replied, "but have you believed in him as a Saviour from sin? You have believed in him as Nicodemus did when he said, 'we know that thou art a teacher come from God,' but have you believed in him as Peter did, when, with the waters giving way under his feet, he cried, 'Lord, save me'?"

He had almost a startled look as I asked these questions, and an embarrassed one at the same time.

"Let me explain what I mean," I continued. "You have been on a long strain of mind this morning. I can see that you are physically exhausted. You want refreshment. There, in the next room is my table, spread with our Sunday dinner. I shall ask you, directly, to go in with me and share our meal, You will believe in the actual existence of the articles of food you see, in their wholesome properties, and in their capacity to relieve faintness and hunger; but if you do not believe in the sense of *using* these articles, appropriating them and incorporating them into your own personality, your faith will, certainly, bring you no relief. Now, Jesus offers himself to men as 'the bread of God which came down from heaven and giveth life unto the world.' The faith which the presentation of bread requires is a faith which applies it as food, which stretches forth the hand and takes and eats it. In such a way, in believing in Jesus, we bring our needs, our sins, our emptiness and our guilt to him, and rely upon his grace and power to relieve and remove them. S——," I said to him, solemnly, for I felt the occasion to be an intensely solemn one, "are you hungering after peace with God, the pardon of sin, and the possession of a truly religious or holy nature?"

He said, "I am sure I am!"

"Do you see in Christ the bread which God has provided to meet this hunger?"

"It seems all clear to me now," was his reply.

"Then take, and eat, and live forever!" I said, springing to my feet in my emotion; and he, with a similar motion and a beaming countenance, responded, "I will; I do!"

"Now, let us pray," I said; and with such sympathy with him as took his soul into union with my own, I commended him to God as one new-born into his family, and besought for him the nurture of the Holy Spirit, that he might be kept in all time to come, building upon Jesus as the foundation of his religion, and feeding upon him as the bread of God.

He declined, of course, my invitation to dine; and we parted at the door, almost in silence, under the consciousness, on both sides, that a great event had transpired in the history of a human soul. My confidence in it, that it was a real transaction, was founded, not so much on the excitement produced by the sermon to which my young friend had listened, as upon the training he had received, the religious experimenting through which he had passed, and the evident sincerity and eagerness of desire for light and relief which his previous disappointment had inspired.

I saw him again, for a moment, at the close of service to-night, and as I clasped his hand, and said, in a low tone, "Is Jesus still the way, the truth and the life?" the warm pressure he gave me, and the bright expression of his countenance were the satisfactory reply.

EXTRACT X.

THE SABBATH SCHOOL.

Sunday, November 10.—I am satisfied that the Sabbath-school will present itself to a thoughtful elder of a church as a legitimate and important part of his domain, and that, in some direction, he will give it a portion of his attention. It is a modern institution only in the sense of being a means of giving religious instruction to the young and ignorant of a community generally, or irrespective of their relation to a church. Immemorially, the children of the church, as all the children of communicants, who had received baptism, were assumed to be, were placed under a course of training in order that they might be prepared, at a suitable age, to ratify their church relationship by coming intelligently and heartily to the communion. They formed a class of catechumens. Unbaptized applicants for membership in the church were placed in the same, or a similar class. The *school*, therefore, may be said to have existed always; although, as it was not necessarily, nor perhaps commonly, confined to the Sabbath as the time for conducting it, it was not called a *Sabbath*-school. Raikes, and the other founders of the modern Sabbath-school, undertook to bring the outlying masses of children who had none to christianize them under the influence of religious culture by bringing them together on the Sabbath, as a day on which they were exempt from worldly labor, for the purpose of receiving instruction. The work was a good one, and in the line of the church's duty, and church officers and members largely engaged in it. Ultimately, and perhaps gradually, the church-school has become absorbed in the Sabbath-school, as the function of the latter seemed to be akin to that of the former. To my mind, this delegation of the oversight of its catechumens has been an unfortunate one. But, inasmuch as it has taken place, it behooves those who have the charge of the Sabbath-school to make it as efficient as possible in supplying the culture which the church owes to its baptized children, and the unenlightened candidates for membership in it. As an officer of the church, therefore, I feel that the Sabbath-school has a special claim upon my services.

For several years I have been a teacher in our Sabbath-school, and have found the work increasingly pleasant. I have taught classes of both boys and girls, and have discovered equal points of attraction in each. I have thought, studied, and prayed hard that I might acquire the art of winning these young souls to myself, in order that I might win them to Christ. I have aimed, first, to impress them with the belief that I felt a personal interest in each one of them, and then to make them feel at ease with me, without losing their respect. There is such a thing, I am convinced, as an organic tie which may be established between a Sunday-school teacher and his class, under the prompting of which the teacher may, with a special fondness, say, "my class," and the pupil, in the same spirit, may say, "my teacher." This tie I have sought to cultivate, and to connect the sentiment which it implies with the practical purpose of giving to my scholars the knowledge of God, in order that they might serve him. Without assuming any special austerity of manner, I have endeavored to impress my class with the idea that in the school-room they were as much in the house of God as in the church; and that my business is to teach them the religion of the Bible, and to persuade them to practice it, as much as it is the minister's. Every now and then I have been accustomed to bring to them some one of the many passages of the Scripture in which the gospel is epitomized, as if I had found a fresh treasure, and set them to commit it to memory and recite it to me. I require each scholar on entering my class to learn and repeat 1 Chronicles xxviii. 9, as a sort of matriculating rite. I think my methods have not been without fruits, for during my teacher-days I have had the joy of seeing some score of pupils connect themselves with the church.

I am revolving these reflections to-night, because my teacher-days are ended, at least for a season. I have been chosen by the teachers, and appointed by the session, to the office of superintendent of our school. This may be promotion and an enlargement of influence, but I foresee in it a serious curtailment of enjoyment. I must cease to use and to hear the terms which have become dear as household words to me—"my class," "my teacher." I must act now very much through other hands. I want to get a definite conception of the work I am to do in my new position.

Certainly, believing, as I do, that the Sabbath-school's right to exist lies in its being an organic factor of the church, its function must be that which the Lord assigned to his church when he said to the founders of it, "Go, make disciples of all nations; teaching them to observe all things whatsoever I have commanded you." It must be a *teaching* institute, like the church. It must be a branch of the church, vitalized by the same principle, and aiming, in all its details, to produce the same result, that is, the making of disciples of Christ. What the preacher and pastor does in his higher sphere, as the instructor of a congregation, the Sunday-school teacher is expected to do in a lower one. He must be the bearer of religious truth to the children of a community, ministering the bread of life to those who come from homes where there are none able or disposed to give it to them.

I am glad to feel that in undertaking the charge of this school I am not engaging in a work which is collateral to, or independent of, that of the church, but one which is normally identical with this, so that I shall be laboring side by side with our minister in the spiritual culture of this field. I shall encourage myself by the assurance that I can claim for the work of this school all the aid and support which Christ has promised to grant to the work of his church.

If, now, I can secure—which I shall endeavor to do—a concentration of spirit and effort on the part of my teachers, in the fixing in these young minds of right ideas of Christ and his religion, I may hope to make of our school an efficient arm of the church, and may safely leave much, as to the methods of instruction employed in particular cases, to the discretion of the teachers.

May the Lord, who has laid this new burden upon me, so guide me in the bearing of it that I may have the joy of gathering many sheaves for his garner out of this interesting harvest-field!

EXTRACT XI.

A REVIVAL.

Sunday, December, 1873.—Our church and community have been signally blessed during the last six months, with what, I think, may safely be called a genuine revival of religion. An interest, amounting to a profound concern, in regard to personal religion, has prevailed to a degree which has made the fact phenomenal. It seems to me that the methods have been legitimate, and that everything extraneous to the simple operation of the truth and the Spirit of God have been excluded. Faithful preaching we have always had, and I believe faithful Sabbath-school instruction. Family training has been pretty well observed in our congregation, and the testimony of consistent living, on the part of a good portion of our members, has not been lacking. These have not been without their results. But special, as well as ordinary, manifestations of the Spirit's power, I am satisfied, we are warranted by the Scriptures to expect and pray for. He who, like the wind, works as he listeth, may evince his presence by the measure, as well as by the form, in which his agency is demonstrated. Nations may be spiritually born in a day as well as men.

Early in the last summer certain persons in our various denominations were led to confer in regard to an effort to awaken thoughtfulness on the part of our people to the claims of Christ to their faith and obedience, and a resolution was adopted to open a daily union prayer-meeting, at an hour preceding the business period of the day, in the lecture-room of our church, which was central and accessible. It was to be under the control of leading laymen of the different churches. No speakers were invited from abroad. Our clergymen were asked to give their presence and aid, exactly as other attendants were expected to do. No unusual services were announced; no choirs were collected and trained; no extraordinary attractions were introduced or advertised.

After notice given in the various pulpits, the meetings commenced on a Monday morning in May last. They were limited to an hour. From the start they were well attended, and the congregations grew from day to day. Leaders from the different churches, chosen by the committee who had the movement in charge, presided in succession. They seemed to be singularly gifted in the way of ordering the exercises and their expositions of the word of God. They kept the tide of thought and feeling moving without a pause, calling for prayers and counsels from particular persons and opening the door for voluntary remarks as any one present was disposed to make them. The hours passed pleasantly and rapidly, and there were few who had been induced to be present on one occasion who did not feel moved to come again.

It soon became apparent that these meetings were having an influence upon the public mind. Multitudes resorted to them who had previously shown no relish for religious exercises. Men who had, heretofore, been fixed in their indifference, or who had stifled their convictions of duty, now felt a fascination which brought them, with anxious faces and unvarying regularity, to the house of prayer. A mysterious power, counteracting the power of worldly things, had gone forth into the community. Religion might almost have been said to have become a theme of popular discussion. Christians were emboldened to propose it, and inquirers were found on every hand to confess their willingness to receive instruction. In several instances it occurred that persons, at the time when free remarks were called for, rose and asked for the prayers of the meeting. No demonstrations of this kind were solicited, and no adjuncts in the way of stimulants to feeling, or tests of purpose, were employed. Whatever personal influence was used to persuade men to embrace religion was used in private conference. That a work so evidently deep and wide-spread should go on so quietly was a marvel.

The interest in our own congregation became so extensive that Dr. N———, in order to meet the craving for instruction which accompanied it, appointed a short daily evening service, in which he might adapt his teachings to the discovered needs of his own flock; and at the close of this, he, with the session, engaged in conversation with such as desired counsel. Many touching incidents attended these interviews. Later on, the session commenced holding meetings frequently, for the purpose of receiving the profession of those who gave evidence of entertaining a true faith in Christ. There was no hurry, no confusion, in this method.

These daily meetings were kept up through the summer. The result has been a decided lifting-up of the tone of the religious life among God's people, and the addition to the membership of our church of about one hundred and twenty souls, and there is every reason to believe that in most of these latter cases the conversion has been a radical one.

One of the remarkable things about this movement is the impression which has been made upon that portion of the community which has not come under its direct influence. There is a silent recognition of a fact which seems to be too patent to be pronounced unreal, although the nature of it is inexplicable to these observers. We hear no words of ridicule, no charges of fanaticism, no questioning of the sincerity or the intelligence of those who have professed repentance for sin and faith in a Saviour. The unexpressed conviction of the onlooking crowd, if put into words, would be, "This is the Lord's doing; it is marvellous in our eyes!"

Such a season of grace, permitting God's children on earth to share something of the joy of the angels in heaven over sinners repenting, calls, it seems to me, for some serious reflections.

First, There is danger in the spiritual sphere, as well as in the natural one, that a rich harvest may invite to indulgence in rest, and a release from the obligation to labor. God has wrought so wonderfully for us, the sophistry of our carnal nature may suggest, that there is no necessity, at least for the present, for our working. I must guard against this fallacy and put our people on their guard against it.

Second, The true view, certainly, is that grace, in showing us the ground of our salvation in Christ's work, instead of absolving the recipient from working, furnishes him with a new and special incentive and encouragement to work. The seasons of langour which, it is said, often succeed revivals of religion, ought not to occur. They are a reversal of the order of God's economy. Grace is in order to life and activity.

Third, These new converts, many of them young, who have come into our Christian family, will need parental care and nurture at the hands of the church. It is a gross inconsistency and an unnatural cruelty to rejoice over a new-born soul and then leave it to starve. These tender plants must be watched, and nourished, and trained; and here I see a large future work for the officers of the church and its maturer members. The wisdom of a Solomon in the edification of the structure, added to the zeal of a David in the gathering of the material, may issue in the rearing of a permanent and glorious temple. And,

Fourth, A revival in a church is illusory if it does not produce a manifest and abiding elevation in the scale of piety in the whole body. The quickening or reviving of a church is to be evinced, not by the numerical magnitude of its constituency, but by the spirit of active godliness which animates it.

God grant that in time to come, when the great Husbandman shall come to look at our now thrifty fig tree, he may find it laden with fruit as well as enveloped in leaves!

EXTRACT XII.

A ROMANCE.

September 12, 1878.—I had occasion, during the last month, while on a business trip to one of our lively western cities, to witness an illustration of what I might call Providence in romance. I was entertained for several weeks at the residence of a Mr. R——— W———, a worthy gentleman who has risen to the position of a foremost merchant in the place. Character and energy have elevated him to comparative wealth, which he has used liberally in gratifying his tastes and multiplying his comforts. His home was a pretty, rural one, on the edge of the city, to which a street-railway line, with a station near by, gave all the advantages of the corporation. It struck me as a model nest for the amiable pair who dwelt within it. It was handsome without being ostentatious, commodious in its arrangements, and adorned to the extent of every reasonable desire. Pleasant prospects opened out on every side, and a spacious lawn in front sloped down to the margin of a picturesque little river, along whose banks a file of giant oaks stood as warders of the grounds.

All these features were interesting to me for a special reason. The master and mistress of this comely mansion were, in a certain sense, my children. At some time near the close of the late civil war, the former, Mr. W———, then a young man of perhaps twenty-one years, appeared in our city as the agent of a company of capitalists in the West, to superintend the management of certain cotton estates which they had leased or purchased. His appearance and manners were attractive, and his testimonials were of an unquestionable character. I was introduced to him soon after his arrival, and found him frank, intelligent, and right-minded. At my suggestion, he became a lodger in the family of a particular friend of my wife, a lady who had been left a widow some years before, without means, and who had supported herself and her two little daughters by taking boarders. Mr. W——— retained his quarters in the household for some two years, identifying himself so completely with the home-circle that a strong bond of confidence and affection sprang up between them. The younger child was about seven years old, bewitching in her beauty, her gracefulness, and her vivacity. In the sweet, spontaneous lovingness of her own heart, she drew the love of all other hearts to her. She and the young lodger became fast friends. He filled for her the place of father, brother, companion, and playmate; she to him was the object upon whom all the ardor of a generous nature, which, during his exile from former associations, seemed to crave an outlet, expended itself.

At length Mr. W———, or Robert, as most of us had learned to call him, having completed his mission, was recalled by his employers. The parting was a hard trial for him and the little Jeannette. But, as we say, sorrow does not lodge long in a young heart. She said little about him—rather avoided allusion to him, but carefully treasured up the keepsakes he had left her. Two years passed in the widow's home, and then God called her to himself. The elder daughter was adopted by a kinsman, and Jeannette was added to our flock. Her nature called for a warm atmosphere in which to grow, and she found it in the tender sympathy we felt for her loneliness, and in the regard excited by her confiding and winning ways. She was a sweet graft on our family tree—one with us, and yet unlike. I gave her every advantage that my own children had had, and with her fine talents and avidity for knowledge she ripened into a cultured womanhood. One peculiarity about her was, that she seemed unconscious of the attractions which every one recognized, and rather repelled than sought admiration or attention. As the result, she confined her shining to the circle of her home, like a jewel shut up in its casket.

In the meantime our young friend, Robert W———, had not allowed himself to be forgotten. Every now and then letters came from him to his little Jeannette. On her birthdays, and at other times, handsome presents were received from him. Occasionally, he sent a picture of himself, and asked for one of her in return. His love for the child retained its place so freshly in his heart that he seemed to be incapable of appreciating the lapse of years and the changes it had wrought, and addressed her in the same frank and hearty way that he had done when she used to clamber on his knee in her mother's home. His letters were full of amusing incongruities when he referred to her, but managed to let us know that he was prospering in business and acquiring both reputation and wealth. Shortly after his return to the West he had connected himself with the Presbyterian Church.

One day a telegram was received from him, telling us that he was on his way South, and would stop and spend a day or two with us. These tidings created a flutter in the household, setting every mind to work at framing conjectures, anticipations, and devices for entertaining our "mythical relative," as we had been wont to call him. He arrived at the designated time, and stood before us with hardly a perceptible change from the image of him left upon our memory when he had vanished from our sight ten years before. There was the same genial air in countenance and manner which used to make him magnetic; the same ingenuousness pervading his address, in which ardor was combined with delicacy, which had marked him in his youth; and as the result, in a few moments we were all as much at ease together as if we had parted only yesterday.

All were, of course, interested in seeing the meeting between him and Jeannette. As hand after hand was rapidly grasped, he came to her, and, almost overcome by his emotion, cried, "Oh, Jeanie! Jeannie! my little one, do I see you again?"

With a smile, placid as usual, she said, "I almost wish I could be a little one again, that you might be sure that it is really I!"

"Oh, no!" he exclaimed, "I see my little one all here and—so much more! You must tell me all about it—how the little one has grown up to be the splendid—well, I mean the woman that she is; but, to me, it will be the 'little one' that I see all the way through!"

He spent two days with us, during which he and Jeannette were much together. The period of time during which they had been separated was reviewed step by step, and by the time he took his departure the two streams of life seemed to have become as closely intermingled as they had been in her childhood.

The evening after he had left, she and I were alone, when, in a rather embarrassed way, she said to me, "Uncle" (I had taught her to call me thus), "Robert, I mean Mr. W——, expects to return here in about a month."

"Well," I said, "we shall all be glad to see him—shall we not?"

"Yes," she replied, "I suppose so; but," she added, in a voice dropping low, if she were almost afraid to hear her words, "he told me that when he came he should ask me to become his wife. He said I belonged to him, that God had given me to him, and kept me all these years for him, and that his life would be a worthless blank unless I shared it with him.

He did not want me to say yes or no then, but asked me to consult with you before I gave him my answer. Oh," she exclaimed, as she finished her communication, "he is so good and kind that I could not be offended with him; but I had not thought of this!"

She was in tears when she stopped. I was not surprised at this revelation; and said to her, "My child, perhaps God has been thinking about it. We must look at the matter religiously. One thing is certain, we know Mr. W―――― to be a man, in the fullest sense, worthy of respect, confidence, and even affection. It is strange that with his many engaging qualities and his social disposition he has not been involved in an attachment with some one long ago. His love for you seems to have kept pace with his years. Don't you think it is real?"

"He says it is, and that it cannot be anything else, for it is a part of his very life," was her reply.

"And don't you think that you have a regard for him, which may possibly be what is called love?" I continued.

"Uncle," she said, looking me earnestly in the face, "beyond you and your dear wife and children, there has been nobody in the world for me to love except Mr. W――――, who has strangely cared for me all my life, I may say, and whose tender interest in me has seemed to unite him inseparably with all my thoughts and affections, although I never thought of it as the love that leads to marriage."

"My dear," I said, "we must lay this subject before God. If his hand is in it, his voice will give an answer to your perplexity. You have time to reflect, and to test your feelings, and to pray for divine illumination. You are God's child, and if you go to him for counsel he will not suffer you to err in your decision."

In due time Mr. W—— reappeared, a favorable response rewarded his devotion; and in a few months later he returned to claim his bride. In the presence of a few friends Dr. N—— united the handsome pair, and in a few hours they left on the train for their future home. As they drove from our door my ejaculation was, "It is the story of Isaac and Rebekah over again!" My wife, amidst her tears, exclaimed, "In thee the fatherless findeth mercy"; and an old colored mammy, who, like her class, was bound to be in the front at a leave-taking, gave vent to her Calvinistic faith in the words, "Sure, de good Lord has been knowin' of it all de time, and has jest been keepin' these dear children for one another!"

It was in the home of this happy couple, the abode of domestic virtue and sanctified affection, that I have recently been sojourning; and as I broke bread at their generous table, it was sweetened by the reflection that it was a fulfilment of the promise, "Cast thy bread upon the waters, for thou shalt find it after many days."

EXTRACT XIII.

A PESTILENCE.

Sunday, November 9, 1879.—The November frosts have brought us deliverance from a deadly scourge, which for the past two months has been desolating this community. Early in the fall the suspicion that several cases of the yellow fever, the occasional plague of our southern seaboard, had occurred, had agitated the public mind. The certainty of the fact slowly revealed itself. The doubts of the most incredulous at last gave way, and then the usual panic ensued. Every one who could find a retreat, near or far, fled. The multitude who could not get away remained to meet their fate, persuading themselves, however, that, on one ground or another, they would be exempt from the touch of the pestilence. I, who had passed through several seasons of this kind, and considered myself acclimated, although I had never taken the fever, resolved, after removing my family to a place of safety, to stay at home and render such assistance as I could in caring for the sick. It has been a time of trying, and, I trust, in many respects, profitable, experience to me.

Nothing can be more depressing than to feel, day after day and night after night, that you are enfolded by the shadow of death. The dreary continuity and monotony with which one has to revolve in thought and conversation such topics as the new victims added to the list of patients, the latest symptoms of those under treatment, and the fatal issue of the struggle in this case or that, are simply awful. Perhaps it is not strange that many persons at such seasons grow reckless, and resort to dissipation as an antidote to the gloom of their surroundings. It is said that while, during the prevalence of an epidemic, the ordinary branches of business are, for the most part, suspended, the saloons and places of revelry are patronized to an exceptional extent. The evidences of the intense, and even brutal, depravity which our fallen nature is capable of entertaining and exhibiting, which have come under my own notice, are astounding. Rapacity seems to leap, like a hungry wolf, upon a prostrate community, and gratify its appetite by extorting gain from its needs and sufferings. A cold-blooded avarice can sit at its desk and calculate how the woes of a plague-smitten community, and even the terrors of Almighty God, can be coined into money.

But I thank God that if these fearful challenges call forth the enmity of the carnal mind to him, on the one hand, they give occasion on the other for beautiful exhibitions of faith, brotherly kindness, and self-sacrificing devotion to duty. Christian men and women have led the ranks of the helpers in this season of general distress, and have been foremost in providing means, devising methods, and personally executing them for the relief of the afflicted multitude. A Spartan band have done a heroic work, and have done it, very largely, under the prompting of the spirit of Christ. It has not been a poetic work, which one might touch with a gloved hand, but one of sheer, homely labor, including the manifold services of the literal nurse, and oftentimes in scenes of squalor and upon subjects uncomely, if not repulsive. It is simply hospital work, without the advantage of the facilities which hospitals afford. One is tempted to ask, What place is there for spiritual ministrations under such circumstances? Often, it has to be confessed, there is none. To the patient, racked with bodily pain, raving with delirium, or sunk in unconsciousness, even the offering of a prayer seems to be an unmeaning exercise. Still, the Christian may find in his own experience that the humane element in his philanthropic work may be spiritualized, as an expression of the faith which works by love to his seen neighbor, through the love he bears to God, whom he cannot see. In Christ's name he may visit the sick, and put the cup of cold water to the thirsty lip, and the thought will awaken in his own heart, at least, motives and affections of an eminently spiritual nature. Certainly, I can testify that during these weary watchings by night and labors by day, I have enjoyed a sense of fellowship with my divine Master, and of the blessedness of union with him, which has rarely been vouchsafed to me elsewhere. The testimony which is given before the eye of the world, that religion is deed as well as profession, is something which also invests even this drudgery of nursing with a spiritual aspect. Then, too, sometimes a soothing word may be spoken, or an allusion be made to the "old, old story of Jesus and his love," which may fall like dew upon a withered soul. I recall an instance of this, which occurred one night as I was sitting alone by the bedside of a man of mature age, who was lying in that stage of exhaustion which follows a severe attack of fever.

He drew a long breath and murmured, "I feel as weak as a child." "Yes," I said, quietly, "God reminds us all sometimes that we are but little children. He would not have us forget the child's trust, nor the child's prayer. Put yourself in the position of a child again, and say, as you used to do at your mother's knee, 'Our Father which art in heaven!' As a little child, Jesus tells us, we must all enter into the kingdom of God. Remember the lessons which were taught you in your childhood; the texts of Scripture, the sayings of the Saviour, the stories of the prodigal son, and of the dying thief, and the hymns which tell of the love of Jesus to us sinners! Oh, yes, it is well for us to be made to feel as little children; for, as men, we fancy that we are too wise and two strong to need God, and so we forget him, and try to live without him; and it is to make us willing to return to him that he throws us back into the weakness of childhood." And so I went on, for I saw that he was not offended, but interested, and soon his lip quivered, and the tears trickled down his face. I paused, fearing that his excitement might be injurious, and asked, "Shall I pray for you?" He gave me an earnest look and nodded his head. When I rose from my prayer, his eyes were closed, but he clasped the hand with which I had been holding his own, which was about the last sign of intelligence he showed. His stupor deepened till he died before the morning. What passed between the Spirit of God and his soul lies beyond human ken; but I am glad I was permitted to say to him what I did.

Our pastor, Dr. N———, has been assiduous in his attention to the sick and afflicted throughout the season. He has kept up, regularly, a morning service on the Sabbath and a weekly prayer-meeting. It has been an unspeakable solace to the limited band who could convene for worship to place themselves thus under the shadow of the Almighty's wings, and to be led out of the arid scenes through which they had been passing during the week, to the fountains of spiritual health and invigoration. Dr. N——— tells me that he is convinced that a minister's presence is needed, during an epidemic, more as a comforter to bereaved households than as a counsellor to the sick and dying.

"Never," was his remark, "have I been more impressed with the perilousness of suspending the soul's salvation upon the chances of a death-bed conversion. While the fight for natural life is going on, there is no opportunity for the religious teacher to interject his instructions. But the poor surviving mourners—their case has touched my heart. Death by the plague is still—death; and for the loved one gone there is the same sorrow as that which floods a family at other times, and the same desire that the precious body should be laid in the ground with the usual testimonials of respect. I am satisfied that, if I have done any good this season, it has been mainly here, in the lifting-up of those who have been bowed down under the strokes of God's mysterious providence."

His remark reminded me of the exclamation of a lady, not of his communion, as she grasped his hand as we were leaving one of these smitten homes: "Oh! Dr. N——, what would we have done in this time of trouble without your counsels and prayers!"

Through God's special mercy, but few fatal cases of sickness have occurred among our communicants. One of these had in it something of the features of a dreary romance, or showed the ruthlessness with which death overrides the tenderest attachments which bind us to life. A young man, a mechanic, who had come from the West a year or more ago, had presented his letter of dismission from a church in his former place of residence to our session, and had been admitted to our communion. His unvarying strictness in observing his religious duties, and his fidelity to all his business obligations, soon gained him the respect and patronage of the community. Under these encouraging auspices, he ventured, last summer, to bring to a neat little home, which he had purchased and furnished, a fair young bride, exuberant in health and beauty as a prairie rose. It was a pleasure, which I frequently enjoyed, to drop in and witness their happiness. When the fever broke out, I begged him to seek some retreat for himself and his wife in the country. He was well, temperate, and occupied with his trade, and his mind could not take in the thought of danger. I repeated my advice the last time I met him on the street. Then he argued that it was too late; that, even if he desired to leave, he must have imbibed the infection. It was, indeed, too late. The next day I learned that both he and his wife were stricken violently with the disease. I hurried to the house, where kind friends had already preceded me, and found him in one room and his wife in an adjoining one, both in a state of delirium—a dull stupor in his case, and a wild rambling of mind in hers. The eclipse which had fallen on his soul was never lifted. Her ceaseless, but irrational, activity wrought like an effervescing fountain. One sentiment seemed to hold its ground amidst all her confusion, and that was gratitude for a little bunch of flowers which I had brought her on one of my visits. She kept them perpetually in sight, talked fondly of them and to them till speech failed her; and when she died, a gentle hand laid the faded emblem of herself on her bosom. The end came to them both on the morning of the fourth day, with the difference of only a few hours in time; and in the shadow of the evening we bore their coffins to the cemetery in the same hearse, and laid them side by side in the same grave. It was the saddest of all the sad incidents I have been called to witness, and an illustration of the instability of human hopes and plans which I shall never forget. We gaze at such anomalies as the Israelites did at the cloud and flame which enveloped the crest of Sinai; and the only solution of the dread phenomenon is to be found in the revelation of the sovereign law, the holy will of the Lord God, which faith discerns through the thunder's voice and the lightning's blaze.

Alongside of this picture is another which is

traced indelibly upon my memory. A young stranger from an eastern State had been appointed by the authorities in charge of our municipal affairs the principal of our public school. The appointment was offensive to our people, and the new officer made no friends. Ultimately the fever seized him. Instantly a tide of sympathy turned to him, and prejudices disappeared in the face of the sufferer's loneliness and helplessness. No effort was spared by men or women to promote his comfort and save his life. I went to his lodgings promptly, and telling him who I was, offered him my personal services, and assured him of the kindly interest felt in his case by the community. He was touched, and became confidential. He told me, among other things, that he was a member of the Presbyterian Church at his home, and had brought his certificate with him, but had been deterred from presenting it to the church by discovering the adverse feeling entertained towards him by the community. He was a recent graduate of a New England college, anxious to teach before studying a profession, and had accepted the appointment offered to him in entire ignorance of the objectionable circumstances under which it had been made. His family had consented to his leaving them in the belief that the opening presented to him was a particularly desirable one.

"Oh," I could not but exclaim, "if you had only gone, as you might have done, to our pastor, and told him all these facts, how much injustice and suffering might have been avoided!" I added, "Everybody is your friend, now. We will do all that human skill and attention can do for you, and Dr. N—— will call to see you, and the prayers of God's people will go up for you." I encouraged him with these and other words.

His attack was a violent one, but his frame was strong, and for a day or two we hoped to see him rally. But the brain began to show signs of giving way, and hope left us. It was devolved upon me to reveal to him his condition. I did so as carefully and tenderly as I could. He looked at me with an expression of amazement and agony on his countenance which was unutterably pathetic.

"Oh, God," he exclaimed, "has it come to this? Was it for this I left my home?" and burying his face in his pillow, he wept and groaned himself into comparative composure. After a while he turned to me again, and said, "Let me speak to you while I can. You will find paper and pencil there," pointing to a table; "take down what I have to say." He gave me the address of his father, and directed me to convey to him numerous messages; "and tell him—tell him," he added, in broken utterances, "Oh, yes, merciful Saviour, may I not tell him—that I died—a Christian?"

He paused a while and then said, "I have one request more. I am engaged to be married. Write to Miss—— ——, at —— (giving me a lady's address), "and tell her that I have loved her to the last, and I think God will let me love her still in heaven. And please put *this* in your letter," he continued, as he drew a ring from his finger. "She will know it, and know what it means!" He was exhausted. I spoke some soothing words, offered up a brief prayer at his bedside, and left him.

I never saw him again. He soon became delirious—frantic, even, and died before the next morning. An unusually large company attended his burial, and women's gentle hands strewed flowers over the stranger's grave. Death called into exercise a charity which, under the mistakes and passions of life, had failed to assert itself. Perhaps there would not be so many sorrows in the world if they were not necessary to keep the fire of humanity burning in human breasts.

Oh, God, how unsearchable are thy judgments, and thy ways past finding out! Surely, it must be that the fascinations of a world which have grown too attractive to me may be broken that I have been called to pass through such scenes!

EXTRACT XIV.

THE GENERAL ASSEMBLY.

June 2, 1880.—Last month it was my privilege to be present as a commissioner of our presbytery at the General Assembly, which met at ———. I had been fairly educated for this office by my frequent attendance upon the meetings of presbytery and synod, but have heretofore declined an appointment to this more august body, partly from a diffidence as to my fitness to do service to the church, but mainly because I could not venture to ask so extended a release from my secular engagements as an attendance upon a General Assembly would demand. This year, as I could consistently command time, I allowed myself to be elected, and was able to fill my seat from the beginning to the close of the sessions of the body.

I confess that it was with a very distinct sense of awe that I found myself associated with this supreme court of the Presbyterian Church. The term "venerable," so often applied to it in the way of courtesy, was to me more than a title; it was a fact. Believing, as

I did, that the idea of the church given in the Bible was correctly embodied in the Presbyterian system, and recognizing the members of this convention as a body charged by the head of the church with the ministerial oversight of its affairs, I had been accustomed to invest it with the highest attributes with which a mere human congress could be endowed. I took my seat in this meeting, therefore, with, perhaps, an extravagant expectation as to the exhibition of dignity, intellectual ability, wisdom and spiritual-mindedness which I was to witness in the proceedings with which, for a series of days, we were to be occupied. These expectations, I am pleased to say, have been to a large extent, gratified. I am impressed more profoundly than I have ever been, with the conviction that our church is loyal to the principles upon which Christ has founded his visible kingdom, that it has realized the right conception of its structure and mission, and that it has been eminently wise in the methods adopted for the execution of its great vocation. If I loved and honored it before, I love and honor it more now, for the confidence I have in it, as true in its adherence to the immutable truths of the everlasting gospel, on the one hand, and singularly adapted, in its working, to the needs and conditions of the world which it is to convert, on the other. I record it as one of the great privileges of my life that I have been permitted to attend this Assembly. I wish to record, now, some of the reflections which have taken shape in my mind, in connection with this pleasant interlude in my experience, before they have lost their freshness.

First, In so large a body I missed the closeness of intercourse, and the warmth of fraternal sympathy with which I had become familiar at the meetings of presbytery and synod. Still, there was a compensation for this loss in the opportunity of seeing the faces and hearing the voices of many with whose names I had long been acquainted, and whose eminence as standard-bearers in the Lord's host had drawn to them the respect and pride which, as a humble member of the same spiritual household, I had been wont to entertain towards these illustrious kinsmen. I have added to the range of my enjoyments in time to come, I am sure, by this enlargement of relationship and affection. It was a thought, too, which often came to me with an inspiring effect, that here, in this company, consisting, for the most part, of men of marked individuality, and representing the diverse mental phases due to sectional environment, and different social and literary training, and who were, yet, all welded together in the closest concord by the inspiration of a common faith in the word of God and a common zeal for the cause of Christ, I was beholding the blessed spectacle of a corporation like that which the apostle describes in his Epistle to the Ephesians, as "a building fitly framed together" and constituting by the unity of its members "a habitation of God through the Spirit." Separate waves they seemed, each possessing its own vitality and maintaining its own independence, and yet moving under the same impulse, and blending in a grand harmony like that of the sea. And as I never look at the sea without feeling that the pulse of God's power is throbbing in its flow, so, in this spectacle, I could not but feel that this confluence of soul was due to the power of God's grace.

There is something, also, of which I am conscious, which I may call the quickening and widening of my individual spiritual life through association with the corporate life of the church, which this protracted communion with so large a body of brethren has awakened in me. Personally, perhaps, I have an increased sense of my own insignificance by having had to exchange the standards of my own little home-sphere for those with which I have been brought in contact during this meeting; but I feel that I am a bigger and a stronger man in faith and in purpose, through the wider horizon which I have been surveying and the stimulating atmosphere I have been inhaling. Yes, I am thankful I went to this Assembly, though I went supposing I was a cipher, and have returned knowing that I am one.

Second, I had no light to throw upon the deliberations of the body through the medium of public address, but I could, and I did, take part in the business by participating in the consultations of several committees of which I was appointed a member. In this capacity I tried to do my best. I soon discovered that a commissioner to the General Assembly was not sent on a holiday excursion. The call for work was incessant, and often interfered with private convenience and bodily comfort. The efficiency of an Assembly in doing business well and promptly lies, I am persuaded, very largely, in the competency and fidelity of its committees. In the rural district where I was born, there were occasional gatherings of the people of the neighborhood at what were called "raisings." A house was to be built. The material for the frame-work of the structure had all been prepared, piece by piece, in the seclusion of the workshop or shed, by the mechanics. When all was elaborated, to the shaping of the minutest pin or brace, the male portion of the community were invited to come and assist in the process of laying, elevating, and jointing the various parts of the building. It was simply a public agency giving effect to a project in which every element had been provided by skilled hands in private. This now obsolete custom, it seems to me upon a review of what I witnessed, might be imitated to advantage by a large ecclesiastical body. Let the work of hewing, planing, and chiselling be done in the committee room, and let the Assembly attend to the *raising*. There used to be, also, a generous feast spread, as the sequel to these gatherings. Perhaps, if the same plan were adopted, there might be a better chance to respond to the hospitable importunities which are apt to pursue the attendants upon our church meetings.

Third, The extent of the work given to the church to do, and the portion of it which it is actually doing, grew upon me immensely, as I listened to the reports of committees, the addresses of speakers—some from mission fields at home and abroad—and the sermons which emphasized the claims of Christ and his kingdom. The apostolic enthusiasm, at which we are accustomed to wonder as an exceptional phenomenon, seemed to me sometimes the most natural thing in the world, to which the heart of the believer in Jesus must open as normally as the lungs of a new-born infant do to the influx of the air, and the real wonder was, that all Christians were not inspired by it. God help me, in all time to come, to be more affected by this sacred afflatus than I have been wont to be!

Fourth, There was something unspeakably refreshing in the thought which often came to me, that I was here consorting, day after day, with a company of men who were animated by a faith in a spiritual world, and influenced by the attractions of spiritual objects. I suppose I was particularly susceptible to an impression of this kind because my manner of life has kept me so constantly under the influence of a secular element. Ordinarily, it is with men who are absorbed with the desire for wealth, and devoted to the pursuit of it, that my position requires me to be conversant. As a man of business, I must talk business, or hear it talked about, from morning till night, until the consciousness of a spiritual nature in myself or others is almost expunged from my mind. Oh, what a relief it was to find myself in a society where the dialect of the market, and the arts of the financier, and the infatuation of money-getting were unknown! Not that these men with whom I was now fraternizing were ascetics who had persuaded themselves that the abandonment of common sense, and the sacrifice of decency and comfort constituted religion, but that in their policy the love of the world was kept in subordination to aspiration after spiritual ends, and things seen and temporal were sought and used only as auxiliaries in the acquisition of things unseen and eternal. On this sordid earth, it was pleasant to find a place where earthly lusts did not intrude, where the prevailing passion was the love of Christ, and truth, and righteousness, and not the craving for riches and social or political eminence, and over which the presence of the Holy Spirit might complacently brood.

Fifth, I must say it was a matter of unfeigned satisfaction to me to notice that the eldership, as a part of the constituency of the Assembly, were a positive and not merely a negative element. They received in a marked way the respectful appreciation to which their rank as presbyters entitled them. I realized from this fact that the church is a "spiritual commonwealth," and not a hierarchy. The popular factor in it was more than a shadow and an echo. It was not unfrequently a perceptible force, and a salutary one, in determining action. As the real aspect of an object may be better ascertained by throwing upon it lights drawn from different quarters, so the acumen and culture of a mind expert in secular problems may be advantageously combined with the skill derived from scholastic research and theological training. There were men on the floor of this Assembly who could see points and bearings in a proposition that had escaped the eyes of spectacled divines. I could not, of course, pose as one of these, and could only sit dumb while the oracles spoke; but I am sure there were some among my brethren in the eldership whose clear vision and practical tact untied for me many a knot in which my mind was entangled, and through their gifts and efforts I felt that the office they held was abundantly magnified.

Sixth, The optimistic view I have been expressing must be toned down a little by two other reflections which I have brought back from this meeting. One is, that the idea of a "dead line," marking the *exitus* of efficiency in the life of ministers, which I hear of occasionally as floating about in the religious community, seems to have insinuated itself, to some extent, into the highest court of our church. It seemed to me, on several occasions during the sessions of the late Assembly, that the elder and more mature men were almost interdicted from taking part in the discussions on important subjects by the forwardness of younger members. At least, the opportunity to speak had to be won by such a struggle, such an outlay of voice, and such alertness of motion in catching the moderator's attention, that the venerable seers, whose conceptions of decorum, probably, had been derived from an earlier age, or whose lung-power and physical agility were unequal to the contest, preferred to surrender their rights and to let the junior prophets take the field. Charitably, I hoped that all these Eldads and Medads were indeed prophets, and that the Lord had put his Spirit upon them; but inwardly and emphatically, I said, "Days should speak, and multitude of years should teach wisdom."

My other criticism was in the form of a question: Must a man's opinions be so identified with his personality, that to dissent from the former is to inflict a wrong upon the latter? It

seemed to me that some of the speakers took
the affirmative view of this question. Perhaps
people generally do. I infer this from the
exhibitions of temper and the caustic retorts
which sometimes marred the equanimity of a
debate. Failure to see the correctness or the
logical sufficiency of the opinions expressed by
one member by some other one had the effect
of a personal affront to the former. Surely, we
are none of us embodied truth. Surely, "wisdom will not die with us," as Job reminds his
opponents. In my humble way of thinking,
the man who cannot bear to have the correctness of his opinions challenged without feeling
that he has suffered a personal wrong which
calls for resentment, has claimed for himself a
position which lies very near to an assertion of
infallibility. I am not qualified to philosophize
upon such a subject, but it does seem to me
that a man of sound mind will draw a line of
distinction between himself and his opinions,
at least so far as to remember that, when he
gives his opinions to me, he is making them
mine in such a sense that I can inspect them,
weigh them in my scales, and form an opinion
of my own as to their worth; and, if that opinion does not accord with his, I am not injuring
him, for it is his gift to me, not himself, whose

merits I am canvassing. When I have seen the fire of passion flushing the cheek and kindling the eye of a debater on a church platform, I have said, If there is wisdom here, there is certainly lacking something which St. James calls "the meekness of wisdom."

EXTRACT XV.

PASTORAL CHANGES.

Sunday, October 31, 1880.—To our unspeakable regret, our old pastor, Dr. N———, was obliged by accumulated infirmities to close his ministry among us. For more than twenty-five years he had presided over this flock, and his path, during that long period, was the progressive one of "the shining light, that shineth more and more unto the perfect day." The spirit of the old hero Caleb was in him, but he could not say, as that stalwart octogenarian did, at the close of his career, "As yet I am as strong this day as I was in the day that Moses sent me." From the time he assumed the charge of this church he made himself one with it, knitting himself to it as an organic element, and, apparently, never entertaining a thought or a purpose looking to a change of location. Nor had it ever entered into the minds of his people to desire a change. A review of his history has much to offer in favor of permanency in the pastorate; and I am satisfied that the general law of the church should contemplate this permanency. But the maintaining of such a permanency assumes that there must be, to a considerable extent at least, a permanency or stability in a congregation; and, unfortunately, in the present day this condition is wanting. Dr. N———, in his latter years, has often remarked to me, sadly: "The world renews its youth in each generation that comes upon the stage. Man has no such successive births, or metamorphoses. He grows only older as the decades advance, until some day he awakes to the fact that the current life of the world has swept beyond him. The place in which he will feel himself more sensibly than in all others a stranger will be his native town, if he revisits it after the lapse of fifty years. He is out of date, out of harmony with the tastes, the modes of thought, the susceptibilities and capabilities of the community around him. I will not allow myself to think that it is a new gospel that the people want, but they do want, I fear, a new way of setting the gospel before them. Even familiarity with the look, manner, voice, and the mental processes and habits of a preacher blunts the edge of his counsels, and benumbs the sensibility of both ear and conscience in the hearer. I am thankful," he would add, "that I have been permitted to hold my ground so long in this field; but, in these changeful times, I do not blame the brother who chooses to make changes in his."

One thing I am glad to say in regard to the retirement of our late pastor: we gave him more than tears at parting; we provided amply for his comfortable support during his declining years.

Such an event creates a sort of crisis in the history of a church. It was new to us, and the session realized the responsibilities which were laid upon them under this unusual condition of affairs. We recognized the fact that a minister is a gift of the Lord; we advised a devout waiting for divine direction, and a continual and general supplication for divine illumination, in the effort to obtain a successor to Dr. N——; we determined that the stated worship of God and the regular operations of the church should be continued without variation. We engaged supplies for our pulpit as we could obtain them, and, in the absence of these, resolved, with such ability as we had, to conduct the public services of the Sabbath and of the week. We gave notice that, in the case of deaths in the congregation, where it was agreeable to the families bereaved, some member of the session would be ready to conduct an appropriate service at the burial. We apportioned the territory of the congregation into convenient districts, and agreed to charge ourselves, severally, with the work of family visitation during the interregnum in the pastorship.

Under this arrangement and a tolerably faithful compliance with it, we have, happily, maintained our ecclesiastical order and activity without a material jar; and, as a crowning blessing, we have been led, as we trust, heartily to agree in the calling of a suitable man, the Rev. S—— G—— W——, to become our pastor. This call was accepted, and to-day, by a commission of the presbytery, Mr. W—— was formally installed over the flock. Our dear old pastor was present, and in most touching terms made the closing prayer, "recommending both pastor and people to the grace of God, and his holy keeping."

As the senior member of the session, I do here acknowledge, with special gratitude, the mercy of God in conducting us safely through this transition state, and enabling us, his stewards, at the close of it, to render up, like Ezra's priests, to our new chief, the vessels of the Lord's house, without loss and without detriment.

EXTRACT XVI.

TRIBULATION.

Sunday, *February* 20, 1881.—I am sitting to-night under the shadow of a great affliction. I am tasting a sorrow the bitterness of which, in multitudes of other cases, I have been called to witness and have tried to soothe, and from which, by the singular goodness of God, I have heretofore been exempt. Yesterday I laid in her grave my youngest child, the sweetest, brightest, most precious link, as it seemed to us, in the chain of our family life and love. She had come, like the evening star, to gild our sunset sky, and make luminous the scenes from which the radiance of the daylight had largely faded. We had often thought, with palpitating hearts, of the pain we should experience at leaving her; we had never, till recently, anticipated the anguish involved in her leaving us. The silence of the house, which every one seems afraid to break; the dreary vacancy, in which every token and charm of home life seems to have been swallowed up; this mockery of occupation, in which we seem to be moving about like spectres; this reserve, which keeps us from looking in one another's faces, lest our look should become tears, and from speaking to one another, lest our speech should end in a sob; this stifling sense of falseness, of unreality in everything about us; oh, this living deadness, which has enveloped us all, is teaching us what the death of the darling of the household means. God help us to learn what it means as a part of the discipline he applies to his own children! This "strange thing," as it appears to the eye of nature, must not be thought a strange thing when surveyed in the light of faith. I must escape from this dark spell of grief. It may beguile me into a presumptuous questioning of the ways of God. I must practice the trust and submission I have tried to encourage others, under similar circumstances, to exercise. Perhaps it was to enable me to do this service more effectually that I have been put through this trying ordeal. If I am a branch of Christ, the "true vine," the purpose of my being such is that I may bear fruit to the Husbandman's glory. I must accept purging or pruning as a part of my culture; and the wise Husbandman cannot err in the form in which he applies it. He who maketh sore can bind up. He has not left me without abundant consolation in my present distress. Blessed be his name; if I have one child less on earth, he has one more in heaven!

My daughter had reached her sixteenth year. She was, literally, full of life; full to the symmetrical completion of her own person, and full in the overflowing sympathy, kindness, and geniality with which she affiliated with every other being. Her natural cheerfulness threw a sparkle over the surface of her life like the phosphorescence on the wave, but beneath there were depths of thought and feeling which she seemed instinctively to shrink from revealing. On this account, while there was evidence that she was living under the influence of genuine religious conviction and principle, she maintained a persistent silence on the subject of her personal spiritual experience, and had, invariably, a refusal to make to the suggestion I often presented to her in recent years, that it was her duty to profess openly her faith as a Christian. I was satisfied that it was the intense awe with which her view of the truths of religion affected her that caused her diffidence; and waited for the time when the seal should be broken and her tongue should utter the confiding words, "My Lord and my God." The time came, but in a way that I had not anticipated.

Early in the spring, while on a visit to the country, she contracted a severe cold, which developed rapidly into lung-disease. The summer was devoted to fruitless efforts for her restoration, and ended in the abandonment of hope, in all except herself. From the mountains, whither we had carried her, we brought our patient sufferer home to die. As often as her strength permitted I bore her in my arms, as I would an infant, from her dreary sick-room to an easy chair in our library, from the window of which she could look out upon the street and draw, at least, the semblance of diversion from the sights which were passing before her.

One morning in December, after she had been exhausted by an unusually harassing fit of coughing, she had desired to be borne to her customary seat, and I had gently placed her there. We were alone. After resting a few moments, she gazed at me with an intense earnestness, and said, "Pa! I don't think I shall ever be well."

The terrible secret which had been long disclosed to us, her friends, and which had been half-suspected, but never uttered by herself before, was now divulged. I had been waiting anxiously for such a revelation. It was time the truth should be recognized by her. With such composure as I could command, I replied, "My child, I do not think you ever will be."

She burst into tears, and exclaimed, "Oh, it is so awful to die and go alone, all alone, to meet God!"

There was a pleading look in her eye as she gazed at me, which seemed to me like the soul stretching out its hands to me for succor. It seemed to say to me, "If you could go with me I would not be afraid to die"; and my heart was responding, "If such a thing could be, I would be glad to go with you."

But we both felt the mysterious bar that separated us here. She had crossed a circle over which I could not pass, within which my arm could no longer sustain her. I could only say to her, "Mary, don't you know God well enough not to be afraid to be alone with him? He has been with you all your days. His presence has been full of tenderness, kindness, mercy and grace towards you. My love to you has been but a faint reflection of his love to you. Does he not say in the Bible, 'As one whom his mother comforteth, so will I comfort you'? Cannot you trust yourself with him as confidently as you have been wont to trust yourself to the care of us, your earthly parents?"

And then I spoke to her of God as revealed

to us in Jesus Christ. I showed her how that awful "glory," the first thought of which had appalled her, had been converted into the soft radiance of love as it beamed from the face of her Saviour.

"Nothing but sin and a refusal to accept Christ as a deliverer from its guilt and power," I told her, "could properly make us afraid of God. What Christ is, God is, to the soul that believes in Christ. Just think of God as Jesus manifests him to you, yearning for his lost children, providing for their recovery, welcoming them on their return, and ask yourself, 'Ought I to be afraid of such a God, even though I must meet him all alone?'"

I talked long in this strain, and an undercurrent of prayer was going along with all that I said.

She listened silently, till I asked, "Mary, do you not believe in Jesus? Do you not love him?"

Then, with a gleam lighting up the languid eye, she answered, "I do; I know I do"; and calmly added, "Pa, I had forgotten Jesus. I am not alone; I am not afraid to die!"

The mist had vanished from the dark valley. She never, from that moment, wavered in her trust. She said but little of her feelings, but showed by her cheerful endurance of her sufferings, and by the serenity which rested, like the sobered light of the setting sun, upon her countenance, that the "peace of God was keeping her heart and mind through Christ Jesus."

Once again, while sitting in her easy chair, alone with me, she said, in a deliberate way: "Pa, I have been thinking about my dying so young, and I am sure God knows what is best for me. I am too weak to meet the dangers to which I might be exposed in the world. It is better that I should go now."

A few mornings before her departure, after a night in which she had had little rest, lifting her emaciated arm from her bed, she cried out, "This poor arm! this poor arm! it is so tired!"

"My darling," I said, "soon you will be where the inhabitant shall no more say, 'I am sick,' and where the weary shall be at rest. Isn't the prospect pleasant?"

"Oh! delightful! delightful!" she answered, with rapture in her tone; and in a day or two more she left us, and went, all alone, to be with God.

That vivid phrase, "alone with God," the cry of a startled soul, has been ringing in my ears ever since I heard it, and I think will live in my memory to my dying day. It shall remind me of the awful presence which is always with me, and with me in such an intimate and transcendent sense as makes all other presences insignificant. I will try to find in the thought of this presence an intimation of the solemn import of death. It is the soul divorced from every other object in the universe to stand "alone with God." All that made up the familiar environment of life retires as man steps upon that unfamiliar territory claimed by death. The foot of friendship, of parental love, is arrested at its border. The sceptre and the hand that wielded it part company there. The conjugal bond which made of twain one is sundered there, and the "one" is riven into the "twain" again. The terms "property" and "owner" lose their significance there, and all to which the dying man gave the title "mine" floats from his grasp into that of another. Every attachment, every interest which made him a part of this world, relaxes its hold. Visibly to the observers, as the ship loosed from its moorings drifts out into the shoreless sea, he is borne farther and farther from the reach and sight of all human associations, and in the great expanse into which he is gliding the mind recognizes nothing but God. The blank caused by the dissolution of all earthly alliances brings out with a distinctness which every one feels the one indissoluble alliance which binds the creature to the Creator. Death is the dying of everything else to man but God; for he survives when everything else perishes.

The overwhelming force of this thought of the *loneliness* of the meeting of the departing soul with God was never so impressed upon my mind as by the pathetic utterance of my child. Such a presence, so dreadfully majestic; such holiness, so infinitely opposed to all human infirmity and sin; such knowledge, from which no fault can be concealed; such power, before which mortal prowess can no more brace itself than the leaf can against the hurricane—who can anticipate a meeting with all this without a sinking heart?

And then, let me remember, that what is true of the moment of dying is true of all life. In the loneliness of death we are only discovering by a change in our point of view what has always existed. For are we not "all alone with God," in our several relationship and responsibility, at every step in our course, as truly as we are at the last? Is he not the one being with whom, beyond all other communings and transactings, we "have to do"?

"Whither shall I flee from thy presence?" asks the Psalmist. God so encompassing man necessarily makes a solitude around him; that is, he so fills the sphere occupied by his presence that nothing else can, or dare, appear within it. When he speaks, the earth is commanded to keep silence. Before him no other god is to live. No object can divide man's trust, or love, or homage, or worship, with God. There is always, amidst the countless associations of life, an innermost circle, closer to the individual than any other by which he is united to the world, in which God is speaking, and in which he reveals himself to sight. And there no other being can be seen, no other voice can be heard. It is the infinite unit clasping the finite unit, a Horeb spot where the Lord meets Moses "all alone." The fellowships of earth may blind the eyes of men to this fact. They may divert their minds from it till the solitude of the death-bed forces it upon their gaze. But they do not reverse the fact. It is still true, that living as well as dying, we are "all alone with God."

Thank God such tremendous thoughts do not exhaust the meaning of the phrase. There is a sense in which solitary association with God becomes a precious solace for the loss and pain involved in the desolating experiences to which life is subject. If God is propitiated towards us, and we can rejoice in the adoption of his sons, what happier condition can be conceived of than to be "all alone" with him? He is the all-sufficient one; and with him, sharing his all-sufficiency with us, what good can we want, what evil can we fear? Surely it is the climax of bliss to be all alone with those whom love has made one with us. We realize then, in all its sweetness, the fact that they are ours, and we are theirs. The Christian, shorn of his worldly wealth, or bereft of the fond companionships which once garlanded his home, is still able to feel, in all the bitterness of his loneliness, that though the vanishing joys, of earth have left him alone, they have still left him "alone with God." Jesus has taught us the blessed secret of so *living* all alone with God that we shall not be afraid even to *die* all alone with him. For he is our propitiation, who has changed for us "the terror of the Lord" into the rapture which can exclaim, "I am persuaded that neither death, nor life, nor angels, nor principalities, nor powers, nor things present, nor things to come, nor height, nor depth, nor any other creature, shall be able to separate us from the love of God which is in Christ Jesus our Lord!"

My thoughts on this sad night have been almost beyond my control. It is not I who am speaking, but a dying child addressing a smitten father's heart. O merciful God, grant that in all time to come the remembrance of my lost darling—my evening star which has set to us to shine in a purer hemisphere—may lead me to live more closely, more truly, "alone with thee!"

EXTRACT XVII.

SESSION MEETINGS.

October 10, 1881.—Our new pastor, Rev. Mr. W———, is very rigid in enforcing upon his co-presbyters in the session their obligations as rulers in the house of God. He gathers us together in monthly meetings, and insists upon regularity and punctuality in our attendance. The meetings are not a new feature in our practice, but the insistance upon fidelity in attending them may be called an innovation or, perhaps, reformation. Our old pastor, Dr. N———, was naturally accommodating, and in his latter years grew lax in his *regimen*, so that our sessional conferences were only occasionally held.

I, for one, feel that I am experiencing the benefit of the new order of things. Mr. W—— finds many matters requiring attention in our system of church work. It is like repairing an old house. The process is a sort of endless chain. Each improvement reveals the necessity for another. Our vigilant moderator always has a budget, of more or less length, prescribing things to be discussed and done, so that our meetings are never idle seasons. There are very few engagements of a secular kind that I do not feel willing to give up in order to be present at these monthly assemblies.

Mr. W——'s method is to combine the devotional with the practical in the conduct of them. We meet as an official, and not merely social body, and, of course, open and close with prayer. Between these prescribed exercises, when some perplexing subject is under discussion, or the serious course our thoughts and utterances have taken warrant it, he calls upon some member to offer prayer, as a plea for guidance, or an expression of feeling. This plan, I fancy, keeps us more sensibly under the conviction that the presence of the Holy Spirit, which we formally ask for at the outset, is a blessing actually vouchsafed to us. Our regular order is—

First, To dispatch matters of business, which are strictly pursued, and, if practicable, brought to a conclusion. Here our shrewd president holds the scales firmly in his hands, and sees to it that no irrelevant weights are thrown into them. I have begun to suspect that a Presbyterian tongue, under the excitement of a debate, needs, like the ship, when "driven by fierce winds," to be "turned about with a very small helm withersoever the governor listeth." I have amused myself sometimes in thinking I could see the peculiarities of the original disciples reproduced, in a small way, in our little circle. To-night we had under consultation the starting of a new mission in a destitute part of our city. The pastor was interested in it, and was pleading earnestly for an effort on the part of our church to supply this spiritually famishing multitude with bread. There was Thomas, listening incredulously, and responding promptly, "Why, Mr. W———, I could as soon believe that we are able to raise the dead as to christianize this people." There was practical and cautious Philip suggesting, "Two hundred pennyworth of bread is not sufficient for them, that every one of them may take a little." There was Andrew, with sympathy in his tone, saying, "I know where I can lay my hand on five barley-loaves and two small fishes. But what are they among so many?" There was his brother, Peter, ready to plunge headlong into the enterprise, regardless of all difficulties and risks, because, he said, "he heard his Master speaking to him out of the dark and bidding him come." There was John, with a glow upon his face, remonstrating tenderly, "Beloved, if God so loved us we ought also to love one another." There was rugged James, hurling out his impatience in the question, "If a brother or sister be naked, and destitute of daily food, and one of you say unto them, Depart in peace, be ye warmed and filled; notwithstanding ye give them not those things which are needful to the body; what doth it profit?" There was Matthew, the financier, saying nothing, but busy calculating in his mind the incomes of various church members and trying to apportion a tax upon each, which might furnish the means required to begin the mission. Others sat silent, staggered by the evident importance of the scheme, on the one hand, and by the apparent impracticableness of it on the other.

Mr. W——— waited till this explosion had exhausted itself, and then quietly remarked, "Brethren, we have forgotten the resources which lie in the hands of him who has said to us, 'Give ye them to eat.' Let us pray over the matter, and take it up again at our next meeting."

Such diversities do not impair the harmony of our intercourse. They impart a sort of vivacity to what is often very prosaic work. They probably make more manifest the spirit of concord which really lies behind them; and they certainly show that charitable friction may be the means of evolving light.

Second, in order, comes what I may call a free conversation on the state of religion in our church. We are, each one, expected to give our impressions of things favorable or unfavorable in this condition, to answer the question from our different points of view, "Watchman, what of the night?" to suggest methods for fostering the good seed and eradicating the tares which the enemy may have been sowing, and, generally, to get such an intelligent conception of the state of our field as may enable us to understand the work which is given us to do.

Third, if time allows, we engage in what I believe is called now-a-days a symposium, in which doctrinal subjects, the action of church courts, the phases of the religious world, questions of ecclesiastical policy, the significance of the signs of the times from the pretentious "higher criticism" down to the right of women to play pastor and evangelist, and of children to lead the crusade of the church against an unbelieving world—all are discussed with results which are often positively edifying, and sometimes possibly mystifying.

One thing I may say gratefully, that at these

conferences, while we are not expected to expose our particular "personal experiences," we are often led to form a better estimate of what our experiences, as spiritual men and office-bearers in the church of Christ, ought to be; and I am satisfied that if the elders of a church, in some such way, "spake often one to another," they would find that the Lord had heard them and graciously blessed their communings.

EXTRACT XVIII.

SOCIABILITY.

November 9, 1881.—I am obliged, often, now-a-days, to admit that the physical frame fails to give support to the behests of the will, and the cravings of the heart, as it has been wont to do in past years. I detect this enfeeblement in many directions. I am made aware of it, perhaps, most painfully, in the dimness which has fallen upon my eyesight, by which the discriminative power of the organ has been impaired. A confused vision makes it difficult for me to recognize readily the persons, even friends, whom I meet on the street. This disability necessarily produces, to some extent, a change of manner, which is not always understood by those before whom it is exhibited. It includes in it an apparent lack of spontaneity, cordiality, or warmth, in my address. It means the absence of a salutation where one was expected, the icy rebuff which chills the kindly glow which was warming another heart, the appearance of indifference to one's kind, which is resented as an offence to itself by a generous nature. It is a feature which, I am sure, is foreign to my disposition and habit. It has thrown an obstruction, which I seriously deplore, in the way of my intercourse with my neighbors. I have always taken pleasure in the thought that I was possessed in a fair degree of the virtue of sociability, and that I was endowed with a good measure of aptness in expressing it. My acquaintance with my townsmen has been large, and there have been few among them whom I could not approach with an air of familiarity and accost in a tone of kindness. This general relationship has been a source of gratification to me, and I have regarded it as a talent which I could use with some effect for the credit, and, perhaps, the propagation of religion. I have heard it related of an old professor in a theological institution, that he used to say to his students, "Young gentlemen, in doing good, don't be afraid of putting too many irons in the fire." This that I am referring to may be a small iron, but it may be the medium of conveying the heat which shall convert ore into gold.

I am sure that an elder in a church will need to have his tools well tempered, and the limbs which use them well oiled with this virtue, in order to be a cunning workman. I have never forgotten a rather brusque salutation I received soon after I was ordained from a lawyer of our town. "Well," he said, "I hear they have been making an elder of you. I am glad I shall now know one of your class of whom I shall not be afraid. When I was a little boy, and a Sunday-school scholar at that, I once got into a brawl, and almost a fight, with a young companion, on the square where we had been playing. Old Mr. B———, an elder in your church, who happened to be passing, rushed at us with a roar, seized me with one hand and my antagonist with the other, shook us, and ordered us off to our homes. The next day my father called me into his room, told me that he had been informed that I had been disgracing myself by fighting on the street, and gave me a whipping. From that time my idea of a Presbyterian elder has been that of a Rhadamanthus, with a scowl on his face, a rebuke on his tongue, and a lash in his hand. I hope you will be a better representative of your order." And so I determined to be, and have religiously tried to be.

I have cultivated sociability. It is unfortunate when it has to be cultivated, and I was blessed in having a large stock of it infused into my natural disposition. But it can be cultivated, and perhaps in every case requires some training and regulating; for if a lack of it be a fault, it may run into a fault through excess. I think I have known some ministers who have depreciated the dignity of their office, and their personal influence, by an undue effort to adapt themselves to every social circle into which they might be thrown. The proper desire to affiliate with a cheerful company may lead a man of lively temperament into what the Scripture calls "foolish talking and jesting," and into such a free use of joke and anecdote as may sink the character of the teacher of religion into that of the humorist. Certainly, there is need for study, even in the exercise of a gift or virtue which, more than all other things, requires to be *unstudied*. The study demanded, I imagine, must begin with a man's own heart and conscience, with a desire to act "worthy of his vocation" as a Christian, and to exhibit at all times that sanctified kindness which aims to do a person good, while it furnishes him with entertainment. It would be a happy attainment if we could always so conduct our intercourse with our fellowmen that it should in every case be followed by the remark which we sometimes hear, "I always feel better when I have been with that man."

I have been a long time in the world, and my association has been with men all my life; and I believe the shrewdest of them will be affected materially by the testimony of their senses in their estimate of those with whom they are dealing. I know it is true, as the Bible says, that a man's "words may be softer than oil," and yet be as deadly as the "drawn swords of an enemy"; and yet every one knows that "words softer than oil" are the genuine symbol of kindly dispositions and are so accepted everywhere. The inner man, the invisible spirit which makes the man, is constantly revealing its states and experiences by the phases of the outer man. A tear, a smile, a frown, a gesture, are exponents to us of great commotions in the soul, and are terms used by us to describe amplitudes and abysses of feeling for which we have no other adequate vocabulary. So, manner, address has its force in life, and is not to be overlooked as a part of the endowment which the Christian worker needs. Sociability, discreetly exercised, will be taken as an index of commendable qualities within the man, and the absence of it will affix a sinister aspect to his character. I have found it, if I am not mistaken, a key to the confidence and good-will of my fellowmen. It has gained for me the credit of being essentially friendly and sympathetic, and on the basis of this conviction they have allowed me, in many instances, to remind them of their faults, and even to urge upon them the claims of religion. Men, when their nature is acting in a healthy way, love to *trust*, as the flower loves to bask in the rays of the sun; and to trust is to give to a thing the validity of truth, and to use it as a true thing. And so, I think, when you can get a person to trust you, specifically as a Christian man, you have gone a considerable way in winning him to an assent to the truth of the Christian religion. Impressions, which are sensible, or which are excited by outward causes, may penetrate to the spiritual region, and awaken convictions and affections which are spiritual in their nature. I do not know that I should be extravagant if I should place a wise practice of sociability among the means of grace. And the young are especially susceptible to the influence of an exhibition of it. They love to be promptly recognized and kindly addressed by older persons; to be called familiarly by their names; to be made to feel that they are of some importance in the eyes of their seniors; and they are strengthened in their efforts at right-doing, and their struggles against temptation to do wrong, by knowing that there are other hearts concerned in their triumphs and their defeats. A warm grasp of the hand may have the effect to withdraw some feeble soul from the pit-fall into which it is about to step, and a cordial reminder of a Heavenly Father's love may apply the check to the prurient appetites of the incipient prodigal.

The word "churl" is an odious one, and the character which it describes is one which assuredly has no affinity with the family of God, and is sadly out of place among the officers of his house. May the Lord forbid that this waning eye-sight, the thought of which has led me into this train of reflection, should expose me, through any apparent neglect of courtesy and kindness in my treatment of my fellowmen, to the suspicion of belonging to the class which it denotes!

EXTRACT XIX.

CHURCH DISCIPLINE.

May 22, 1882.—At several of our late meetings of session we have been painfully confronted with questions touching the exercise of discipline in our church. Certain cases of irregularity in the walk of some of our members have been brought to our notice, some of which we are constrained to believe are true. It is not pleasant to deal with these offenders, even in the way of rebuke and admonition, which we all admit to be proper. For this, we have made provision, and have reason to hope that, in some cases, our kindly remonstrances have been effectual in abating the evil. Others seem to some of our number of such a flagrant character as to call for judicial action. We have stood at the door of this appalling procedure for months without venturing across the threshold. We have sighed over the faults of our erring brethren. We have deplored the scandal inflicted on the church by their malfeasance. We have said something ought to be done to vindicate the credit of religion and maintain the purity of our household life. We have heard the voice of the great Lawgiver, saying, let the man who will not amend his wrong-doing upon private intercession, nor upon the judgment of the church, "be unto thee as a heathen man and a publican," and St. Paul saying of the unclean man at Corinth, "Put away from among yourselves that wicked person." We have studied the fifteen chapters and forty-three pages of our *Book of Church Order*, prescribing the "Rules of Discipline," and our minds are staggered at the terrible task that seems to be set before us. The sentiments disclosed by our discussions have shown a disposition to evade, if possible, the stern requirements of these rules of discipline.

At our last meeting, when this subject was under consideration, one member remarked, "To my mind these rules are bristling all over with the terms and technicalities of a criminal code. They suggest the methods of a "court of assize" rather than those of a council of saints. Such words as "indictment," "citation," "prosecutor," "accuser and accused," "offence," "censure" and "excommunication," seem strangely out of place in the law of a spiritual commonwealth; and I confess that only some desperate necessity, like that which calls for the use of a surgeon's instrument, could reconcile me to the processes they describe."

Another expressed himself in this wise: "The execution of these rules is an impossibility. You have no authority by which you can enforce them. Your criminals and your witnesses will laugh at your citations. You have no state now backing up church courts with threats of fine and imprisonment. The day when the ghostly power of Rome could bring monarchs to a bishop's feet is past. The democratic spirit of the age is revolting against the claim of rulership wherever such revolt is possible. The man who has allowed himself to become defiled with an 'offence' is not likely to consent to have his fault publicly exposed; nor is he likely, as it seems to me, to be reformed by being so disgraced."

A third objected to church trials on the ground that they almost invariably produce discords and resentments by which the whole body is injured, and particular members, perhaps, fatally damaged; and sustained his objection by the householder's answer to his servants in the parable of the wheat and the tares, that they should refrain from attempting to gather out the tares, but rather should let both grow together until harvest, lest in the endeavor to rid the field of the tares they should "root up also the wheat with them." "It is poor policy," he added, "to blow up your house with dynamite in order to purge it of the filth that had got lodged in some of its closets."

A fourth was of the opinion that the Saviour had given us a clear intimation of a distinction between the spirit of his economy and that of the Mosaic law, when, in the Gospel of John, chapter viii., he said to the adulterous woman, who by the latter would have been stoned to death, "neither do I condemn thee; go and sin no more."

Still another observed that, to his view, the scandal from which it was proposed to relieve the church by the prosecution of offenders was an imaginary rather than a real object. "For," he argued, "if the scandal lies in the detriment which is done to the good character of the church, it amounts to nothing. Every fair man knows that a heresy or an immorality is not a normal index of the character of a church. The very fact that it is marked as an irregular and reprehensible thing shows that it is at variance with the recognized character of the church and with the nature of religion. The presence of a few black sheep in a flock would not prove that the breed was not specifically white; and those who point to an intemperate or dishonest man in a church and cry, 'See what these Christians' pretensions amount to,' know that they are uttering a fallacy, and that these exceptional types are not genuine representatives of Christian character. The crooked limb is noticed because of its diverseness from the general symmetry of the tree; and further," he added, "I very much suspect that the heated tempers, the indiscreet words, the collisions of feeling which are apt to be engendered by a church trial, may produce scandals possibly worse in virulence and more lasting in duration than those which the court was called to avert."

Evidently, the drift of opinion at our protracted conference was not leading us to any practical conclusion. And after each one had contributed his share to the fog in which we were involved, our clear-headed pastor closed the discussion, and gave us a little tangible ground to rest our minds upon in a short address. "Brethren," he said, "it has seemed to me that the jurisprudence of our church has been under trial to-night rather than offenders against its morals or its doctrinal standards. I wish a judicial system, free from the objections which have fallen like a fusilade from your lips, against our present one, could be devised. But the law has been made for us, as a church, by those who were authorized to make it, and we have accepted it. Until it is changed by a similar authority, we must abide by it, and try to maintain it. There must be a law in all organized bodies. It is the principle upon which their corporate life depends. Our church is right in asserting a power of jurisdiction as a part of its function. This includes in it the right to suppress, as far as it can, whatever is fatal to the existence of the church, provided the methods are sanctioned by the word of God. Extreme discipline may be administered in extreme cases. The exercise of it must be justified by an obvious necessity. This idea is recognized in our *Book of Order*. It teaches, just as distinctly, that discipline is never to be administered in the spirit of wrath or of personal animosity. The motives must be fidelity to the church's head, and love for the souls of its members. The rules we have been commenting upon are really meant, by the precision and amplitude with which they are stated, to make plain the intricacies of a delicate procedure, to avoid embarrassment and mistake, and to secure, as far as forethought can do it, complete justice to all the parties interested.

"My private desire would incline me, perhaps, to simplify methods of adjudication and to dispense with much of the harsh terminology and rigid formality which now give to a church court so much the look of a secular criminal tribunal. Especially would I like to see these family grievances disposed of more strictly within the family walls, and the humiliating exposures involved in the trial of offenders and the infliction of censure eliminated from our practice.

"Happily for us, my brethren, I honestly do not see, in any of the cases brought before us, that there is a necessity for a resort to the painful extremity of a judicial process. We may safely wait for a return of a right mind to our delinquent brethren. We can yet pursue them with our kind expostulations. We can yet pray for their recovery from their wanderings. In the meantime, there are, possibly, some faults of our own, which the consideration of our present trouble may properly bring to our attention.

"First of all, let us ask if the lapse of these fallen kinsmen might not have been averted if we had been vigilant enough in noticing the beginnings of their decline, and prompt enough in going to them with our fraternal warnings and admonitions. The elders, who are among the people, should show their fidelity as watchmen by watching closely over the first haltings of the weak and tempted disciple, and checking his downward way before the momentum has become irresistible.

"And second, may we not learn a lesson as to caution in receiving members into the church? I am convinced we are betrayed into an error by our zeal to witness numerical accessions to the memberhip of our churches. Quality, not quantity, is the thing to be looked at mainly in gathering materials for the upbuilding of the kingdom of God. A spiritual temple grows only by the addition of 'lively stones.'

"'Third, Let us remind one another, as we separate, of the prophet's counsel, 'If the watchman see the sword coming, and blow not the trumpet, and the people be not warned; if the sword come and take any person from among them, he is taken away in his iniquity, but his blood will I require at the watchman's hand.'"

"Now, let us pray and be dismissed!"

EXTRACT XX.

SOVEREIGN GRACE.

Sunday, August 10, 1884.—My services have been required recently in administering counsel in a case of spiritual need, where extreme delicacy was called for in the method of address, and where the result has been, to all appearance, signally gratifying. Believing, as all Bible Christians must, that there is a birth of the Spirit as real as is the birth of nature, many of us, probably, are still wont to couple with our belief of the fact a conception as to what the mode of it ought to be, and to found this conception on the precedents which religious biographies have presented to us, or on conclusions drawn from the so-called laws of mind. There is an overlooking here of the illimitable scope of the operations of such an agent as the Holy Spirit, a fault of which the Saviour forewarns us when he draws a parallel between these operations and the movements of the wind blowing "where it listeth." I have received a great enlargement of vision on this subject by what I have been called to witness. Salvation, in the case of a sinner, is the result of the pure grace of God. It must be so, because the sinner is not entitled to it, and God is under no obligation to grant it. How many precious hopes in regard to the departed are born of this doctrine! The exercises of a dying hour are not always illusory. Grace can perform its regenerating work whenever and wherever God is pleased to bestow his mercy. It is the height of presumption for living men to hang their hope of salvation upon the opportunities of a death-bed, but it would be limiting the grace of God to deny that even upon this extreme field it can achieve its victories and win its trophies.

The case which has awakened these reflections was that of a young man who was to-day carried to his grave. I was doubly attached to him because his father, deceased some years ago, was my particular friend, and because I had seen his youth spring up into a maturity of almost chivalric proportions. In person he was well-formed and graceful, with a handsome countenance and a winning address. Good social position and adequate means had furnished him with refinement and culture. With the avidity of an enthusiastic nature, he saw and coveted the enchantments which lay everywhere within his bright horizon. Every avenue which stretched before him was begirt with flowers, and every flower sparkled with a dew-drop. It was the spectacle of a young eagle waving his burnished wing in the morning sunbeam. In such an element it is not strange that serious reflections were banished, and the restraints of religion discarded. He was gay, worldly-minded, but not vicious. The cup of earthly pleasure mantled so brightly in his hand that in the rapture with which he quaffed its contents he discovered no evil in the draught, and felt no need of a higher good.

No one dreamed that there was an arrow making its way unseen through the air towards this "shining mark." But it was so. Just as he approached the point of manhood, a blight, from some subtle source, revealed itself in that goodly frame. Organic troubles of a complicated sort began to make alarming havoc of its beauty and its strength. He struggled against the mysterious foe, wearied himself in seeking, in every quarter, medical aid and in visiting health resorts, till heart-sick with prolonged disappointment, he turned his feet back to the seat of home-life and sympathy. All others saw that he must die. From his own eye, as is common in such cases, the issue was concealed; and the rally, the rebound into health, was, almost to the last, the object of his definite expectation.

He desired my visits and I saw him frequently. I deemed it most proper, in my earlier interviews with him, not to dissipate his hopes of recovery. I preferred to present the subject of religion to him as something connected with life, rather than as a mere antidote to death; and it gave me special confidence in the genuineness of the convictions and feelings afterwards expressed by him that they were not forced into existence by the terror of the apprehended catastrophe. In my endeavor to introduce the subject to him I found, to my surprise, that the work, to a great extent, had already been done. "My sickness," he said to me, "has been sent upon me to make me think of God and see the folly of a worldly life." And then he added, "There is more than folly in such a life—there is sin."

Conscience, enlightened by early religious instruction, or rather, let me say, the Spirit of God, had been busy revealing to him his guiltiness under the law of God, and preparing him for a recognition of his need of Christ as a Saviour from sin and the appointed way to the Father. In that venture of faith by which the soul rests upon Christ in these characters, by a conscious act of appropriating confidence, he hesitated for a while, but only for a while. The darkness in which, for a time, he groped, yielded easily to a presentation of the doctrines and promises of the gospel; and gradually, as the dawning light, the assurance, "Jesus loves me, even me," took possession of his heart. Henceforth, the expectation of a return to the world which he still cherished was coupled with the desire of consecrating his life to the serving and glorifying of his Saviour.

"You will not be ashamed of Jesus, if God spares you to mingle again with your friends?" I asked.

"No," was his emphatic reply; "I want to live that I may testify of him."

The fatal crisis came sooner, and more abruptly, than any one had anticipated. Every one about him was startled when the sudden premonitions announced its approach. He alone was calm. In an instant, without a struggle or sign of regret, the hope of life which had buoyed him was surrendered. "I am dying," he said, "but I am ready—I am willing;" and then added, "send for the doctor, that he may relieve me of suffering. But Christ is with me, and will bear me to the bosom of God." As an aged relative, whose deafness prevented him from hearing his whispered utterances, approached his bedside, he lifted his arm and pointed upward. Fearing that his gesture had not been understood, he added, "Tell him I am going to heaven, redeemed by the blood of Jesus."

His remaining hours were spent in giving expression to his parting wishes and counsels, and when all was done he said to a beloved friend who was bending over him, "Now, pray that God may let me pass away in unconsciousness or sleep!" And turning his face from the weeping throng before him, in a moment he lapsed into a repose as gentle as an infant's slumber. Whether he was unconscious or asleep, no one knew; but all felt, when, a little after, the spirit was known to have gone, that the pitying Father had heard the cry of his child, and sent the dread messenger to do his work with a veiled face and a muffled footstep.

To us who saw this history evolving itself in its successive stages, the conclusion was irresistible and was spontaneously expressed, "This is none other than a literal verification of the wonderful declaration, 'As many as received him, to them gave he power to become the sons of God, even to them that believe on his name; which were born, not of blood, nor of the will of the flesh, nor of the will of man, but of God.'" A divine power, prior to, and apart from, all human agency, we had not a doubt, had wrought at every step in showing this soul the path of life. And grace, so great and so condescending are the tender mercies of our God, had deigned even to cause the harsh gate of death to turn on noiseless hinges for the exit of this trembling "little one."

Surely, I may adopt with renewed confidence the apostle's creed, "By grace are ye saved, through faith; and that, not of yourselves, it is the gift of God."

EXTRACT XXI.

SPIRITUAL COMMUNICATIONS.

Sunday, March 1, 1885.—We had a sermon to-day from our pastor, which has been to me unusually rich, both in instruction and in suggestion. It was from the text, John xiv. 26, "But the Comforter, which is the Holy Ghost, whom the Father will send in my name, he shall teach you all things, and bring all things to your remembrance whatsoever I have said unto you." It was clear, like the view one gets from a mountain top, in the revelation it gave us of the field which lay within the limits of our vision; at the same time it showed us, in the spaces beyond, vast stretches of heights and depths, which we could only dimly descry. It has brought to my recollection some facts which have lately come under my notice, and which have led me into a good deal of serious reflection, and, perhaps, I might add, speculation.

An excellent lady, whom I knew and esteemed very highly, both for her personal charms and for the ornament of a bright Christian character, had been prostrated for a long time with a pulmonary affection, in a city south of us where she resided. Her husband was engaged in mercantile business, and was required frequently in the interests of his house to make excursions into the interior of the country. Her decline was so gradual that he felt at liberty to continue these excursions, notwithstanding her illness. During his last absence her symptoms had become alarmingly worse, and she had gone to her bed, as was supposed, never to leave it alive. About the same time intelligence arrived that Mr. C———, the husband, had been attacked violently with pneumonia at a little railway station where his journey had led him, and had been conveyed, in a very critical condition, to the residence of some relations in the vicinity of our city. The news of his illness was cautiously revealed to Mrs. ———. She divined at once the import of it, and announced her purpose to go to her husband. The physician and attendants declared the project impossible; but she confidently affirmed that the Lord would give her strength, and directed preparations for her journey to be made. Supernaturally, as it seemed, strength came to her, and she made the journey, partly by steamboat and partly by carriage. It was after her arrival that I first visited the afflicted pair.

Mr. C. had been a man of moral habits, but so devoted to his secular pursuits that the subject of personal religion had never attracted his attention. To my surprise, on entering the sick-room, I found the wife, emaciated in form but full of energy and apparently unconscious of her own infirmities, performing, almost solely, the office of nurse to her husband. He was utterly prostrated, could hardly turn his head, and could speak only in broken and whispered sentences. Mrs. C. was singularly cheerful in her manner, and after telling me of the marvellous support she had experienced in coming to her husband, said, "I knew my place was here, and something within told me that God would hear my prayer and enable me to come. I have a mission, I think, to lead Herbert to Christ."

This introduction made it easy for me to present the subject of religion to the sick man at once. I did so, and spoke simply of the needs of a sinful soul, of the provision which God had made for these needs in the gospel, and of the gracious way in which salvation was offered to sinners through faith in Christ. He listened silently but attentively, and with rather a distressed look, remarked, "I am too weak to think much of these things now, but I will try to. I know they are important, and I believe they are true."

I only added, "You have one with you who has not only professed religion, but lived it; and she can teach it to you better than any one else. She has prayers laid up in heaven for many years for you, and is waiting to see them answered."

I saw him almost every day for the next two weeks, and while receiving no decided expression of his faith in Christ, I was sure I saw signs of a penitent and believing spirit in him. His wife shared with me in this opinion, "but," she would exclaim, "I long to see him have the comfort of an assured hope of salvation!" A night or two before his death, as she told me the next morning, after lying quiet for a long time, he called her and asked, "Did you speak to me?"

"No," she said, "I thought you were sleeping."

"I have not slept—I have not been dreaming," he replied, "but I heard a voice saying to me, 'Go in peace, thy sins are forgiven thee!' could it have been Jesus?"

"Yes," she cried, "I am sure it was Jesus speaking to your soul."

"And then," he continued, "I heard songs away up in the sky, giving God glory for a sinner who had repented. Could this have been the angels rejoicing over me?"

"Oh, yes," she replied, "and your wife rejoices with them."

His face was placid as I approached him, and stretching out his hand to me he said, feebly but distinctly, "I have given myself to Jesus, and he has saved me!" And there was another one added to the rejoicing throng. I felt in that chamber that I was standing "quite on the verge of heaven." His peaceful frame continued till he passed away; and his faithful wife, having seen her mission accomplished, and his body laid in the grave, returned to her home, and, I have learned, speedily relapsed into her former diseased condition, and followed her husband to the home of Jesus and the angels.

Was this a freak of delirium, or the hallucination of a fevered brain? There was no evidence of an abnormal condition of mind, but, on the contrary, every appearance of sobriety. He was not constitutionally imaginative. He had been remarkably calm throughout his sickness. He made no allusion to his revelations in talking with me, and clearly showed no disposition to parade them. I have no philosophy to apply to the facts; but in my simple way of thinking, I am more than willing to believe that, on that border territory that lies between the earthly and the spiritual spheres, there may be such an overlapping of the two, that communications from the spiritual side may be given, and a capacity to receive them developed, on the earthly side, by means of which, things which the natural eye cannot see, and the natural ear cannot hear, may be revealed to a soul withdrawn, for the most part, from the conditions of the earthly sphere and entering upon those of the spiritual one.

In my reading I have met with the phrase, "the *sub-conscious* states of mind." The truth conveyed by the phrase, if there be a truth in it, lies so far beyond and above my plane of thinking, that I am afraid to say that I have a definite conception of it. I fancy that it assigns to the mind, or the spiritual self, a department which is under or deeper than the ordinary seat of consciousness. It does not yield us the ordinary phenomena of consciousness, but possesses a capacity to respond to forces of an extraordinary sort, and gives us a consciousness of things which lie beyond the reach of natural apprehension. It is a region of potentialities which may come into acts under special inspirations. Perhaps I may liken it to an instrument of Æolian strings, a hidden harp, lying in a chamber of our spiritual nature, which is silent, unknown, till the breath of some extraordinary breeze wakens it into sound, voice, or song. Spiritual fingers touch these strings, and, lo! we see visions, and hear music, which we never saw or heard before. The fact appears, possibly, in regeneration, when the new-born soul expresses itself in such utterances as these: "One thing I know, that whereas I was blind, now I see"; and "old things are passed away; behold, all things are become new."

Now, may not the spirit, just hovering on the confines of heaven, get communications of heavenly things which transcend any which can come to it from the earthly side? Through this mysterious sub-consciousness, may not Jesus speak to his departing follower, and the angels' minstrelsy float down to his ear? I feel afraid to affirm and afraid to deny. But I must say, it is infinitely pleasant to me to believe that heaven thus stoops down to cheer the pilgrim as he enters its radiant atmosphere, and that John Bunyan was not wholly dreaming when he made Christian, as he approached the Celestial City, see "shining ones" sent forth to cheer and support him, and hear "all the bells of the city ringing" to give him welcome, and the melodious noises of the King's trumpeters "making the heavens to echo" with their congratulations at his victory. This picture may be but the creation of a poet's fancy, but I must confess to a wish that it were true; and to a sympathy with Bunyan when he gazes enraptured at the glories of his vision and wishes that he were "among them."

By a strange coincidence, I met, a few days after the death of Mr. C———, a case somewhat similar here in town. A friend of mine, a man of some forty-five years of age, a scholar, and a professor in an institution of learning, was in the last stage of consumption. He had been confined to his room for months, during which I often visited him. His tastes were refined and his habits correct. He made no pretension to religion, in the ordinary sense of the word. In a sense of his own, perhaps, he called himself a religious man, for his fault was self-reliance, or self-conceit. He used the phrases, "I think," "I believe," as if his opinions and beliefs settled for him the right or wrong of any proposition. His mind was an active one, and he prided himself on his independent use of it. Respect for social opinion led him to be a supporter of Christianity, and an occasional attendant upon the preaching of the gospel. Our pastor was accustomed to say of him, that he always felt, when he saw him among his hearers, that he came clad in a coat of mail, so compact and polished that every arrow he could aim at him must glance off without leaving a dint.

I liked his company, and found his conversation, on most subjects, instructive. In my visits to him after his confinement to his sick-room, I was careful, in my way of expressing myself, to assume that the accepted opinions of Protestant Christians were the truth, and to avoid being led into a discussion upon them. He was too courteous, generally, to introduce one. He expected to get well, for he had reasoned himself into the conviction that he ought to be, and so must be. As time passed on, there was an evident decline in his confidence, and a growing seriousness in his view of things. I ventured, after one of our interviews, to propose prayer, and his reply was, "Do pray for me, for I need it." I asked him if he would receive a visit from our minister, Mr. W———, to which he said, "Of course; tell him I shall be glad to see him."

Mr. W—— became interested in him; and in his usually discreet way, after he found that his presence was agreeable to him, urged upon him the claims of personal religion. He frankly stated some of the views he had been wont to hold upon this subject, to which Mr. W—— only replied, "Professor, my study and my experience, too, have taught me that I am simply an empty vessel; and that God is the fountain from which I must draw my supplies, if I would know the truth. Considering that, from the very constitution of my nature, I must have the truth in order to be safe in this life, or in any other life, I do not count it a strange thing that God has furnished me with light in his word, and that that word has come to me through the medium of a divine revealer, such as Jesus Christ claims to be. I have taken my little bucket and gone to the fountain thus opened to me, and I am sure that every need has been met, every condition of my well-being supplied, till the efficiency of the provision, consciously revealed to me in daily experience, has become to me the best demonstration that its contents are, indeed, the water of life."

The sick man only remarked, "I believe you have done wisely. Look at me, a poor dying imbecile, with a thousand tormentors preying upon every fibre of my body, and yet unable to prevent or arrest one of them! Shall such a creature talk of being sufficient unto himself? Yes, sir, I congratulate you!"

"My dear friend, will you not go and do likewise?" was Mr. W———'s reply, as he left him.

It was not long before the humbled scholar confessed the folly and sinfulness of his self-idolatry and rejoiced in the revelation of Christ his Saviour God, as the fountain whose fulness could satisfy his every need. He was at his own request baptized, and subsequently, in company with a few friends, sealed his faith by partaking of the memorial supper of the Lord.

The morning of the day on which he died he said to me, "I don't know what to think of it, but it has seemed to me that my sainted mother, who gave me to God when I was born, and never ceased to pray for me, has been with me all night. I knew her, she looked so natural, and yet so strangely bright and beautiful. Was it an illusion? It did not seem so to me. And the sight of her has made me happier than ever and anxious to go to her."

"Believe it was real, my friend," I replied, "if it was an illusion, it was a prophecy. She is waiting for you, and God is telling you that you shall be a little child again, by her side, in your Father's house!"

These incidents, and the long list of similar ones in the annals of the saints, have been of unspeakable comfort to me, in abridging the space between the material and the spiritual worlds, and in suggesting, at least, the possibility of communication between them. And, hereafter, when I read or sing Bernard's, the monk of Clugny, wonderful hymn—

> "O mother dear, Jerusalem,
>   When shall I come to thee?
> When shall my sorrows have an end?—
>   Thy joys, when shall I see?
> O happy harbor of God's saints!
>   O sweet and pleasant soil!
> In thee no sorrows can be found,
>   No grief, no care, no toil,"

I will feel that the dear celestial mother country has become more dear to me because I am permitted to believe that she sends forth her "ministering spirits" to sing her songs to her children just falling asleep in Jesus, and allows the glorified human mother to come into the darkness of the dark valley to welcome a son to the realms of the heavenly glory.

EXTRACT XXII.

THE EVENTIDE.

Wednesday, December 24, 1890.—To-day I commence my eightieth year. I recognize in many of its particulars the correctness of the pictorial description of old age in Ecclesiastes, chapter xii., especially in regard to the bowing of the "strong men," and the darkening of the "windows." The limbs have lost their vigor and elasticity, and dimness has materially impaired the outlook of the eyes. On account of this latter infirmity, I shall have to abandon this practice of noting the events which have arrested my attention and awakened reflection in my humble life, or call in the aid of an amanuensis, which, I fancy, would interfere with the freedom with which I have been wont to indulge in my lucubrations.

I wish, at least, before I lay down my pen, to make one more indorsement of the inspired record that "the Lord is good, and his mercy endureth forever." He has certainly dealt kindly with me, and the blessing which has given peculiar value and sweetness to all other blessings is the knowledge that all my blessings have come from him. It is religion which has made my life a happy one, in the absence of most of those adventitious adjuncts upon which men commonly depend for such a result. I have been under the necessity of constant labor; I have been thwarted in many of my schemes for bettering my worldly estate; I have been constrained often to undergo self-denial; I have suffered the fretting anxieties of household care, and I have felt in all its keenness the anguish of bereavement. Yet I have enjoyed the great boon of a definite and reputable occupation; I have had almost uninterrupted health; I have known the wholesome comfort of contentment, if not the luxury of gratified ambition; I have broadened a very contracted life by the sympathies with which I have entered into the lives of others; I have come to see that privations were safeguards against the snares of temptation, and afflictions the chastenings which have brought me to a sense of my faults. Somehow, as I review the long pathway I have trodden, and the scenes through which it has conducted me, I can see how the pillar of fire and cloud, the signal of a divine guidance, has been with me at every step; and, in the light of this fact, I am assured that my journey will not fail to reach its promised destination, in the rest prepared for the people of God.

He who blessed the house of Obededom, because the ark was within it, has blessed mine. Harmony, unselfishness, and affection have made us, literally, a united family. I have had five children. One is not, for God chose her to be the first-fruits of the flock in heaven. My oldest son is married and living near me, and his little ones cluster about me as autumnal blossoms sometimes come to deck the nakedness of an old tree. The younger is a student in college, and my hope is that he may be called of God to enter the ministry. My eldest daughter is happily married, and lives within easy reach of us, at the town of P———. The last one, who was appropriately named "Ruth," is my guardian angel, whose devotion to me all her life has been saying, "The Lord do so to me, and more also, if aught but death part me and thee;" and whose persistence in declining all other alliances has shown her determination to execute her vow. Since the death of my wife, six years ago, she has presided over my home, and done all that filial love was capable of, in healing the aching numbness of my dissevered life. All my children are communicants in the church.

For the last two years I have retired from active business, and removed to a modest little cottage on the outskirts of our city, where, in a quietness which I profoundly enjoy, I await the hour when my sun, like the natural orb, which I watch so often from my front piazza descending to its rest in the western sky, shall sink below the earthly horizon.

The retrospect of my life, in which, like most persons in old age, I find myself often engaging, leads me to many and varied reflections. One is, that my life has been sadly unproductive of those fruits of holiness and usefulness by which God is glorified by his servants. The things of the world which so absorb our vision in our earlier years contract their dimensions and lose their lustre immensely as the great things of eternity loom up before our gaze; and we wonder, as we look at them from the standpoint of a Christian faith, that we could ever allow their attractions to outweigh the claims of the kingdom of God to our thought and labor. The obligations we are under to the divine Master, who, though he was rich, for our enrichment became poor, seem so immeasurable as we think that this enrichment is soon to be revealed to us, that, like the publican, we cry, "God be merciful to us sinners"; and with an ardor in our trust, simpler and stronger than that with which we first came to Christ, we lay hold of his righteousness and hide our deformity under his mantle, graciously presented to us in the gospel. We may modify our self-reproaches by reminding ourselves that our talents have been few, and our sphere of influence limited, but the disposition to make such excuses will soon vanish before the stern conviction that we have fallen short, in many ways, of that perfect consecration to Christ which he requires, and which he deserves.

Still, I have comforted myself by reflecting that I know that my life as a Christian has been under the control of a new law and a new principle; and that amidst all the intrusions of the fleshly mind I could say, as Peter did, "Lord, thou knowest all things, thou knowest that I love thee." There is a satisfaction in the performing of a religious service, which is distinct from any which we may derive from the thought that we are doing good, or even from the thought that we are getting good. It is a feeling akin to that pleasant one which we derive from any bodily exercise which indicates physical health, as the joyous note of the bird gets its tone from the joyousness of a sound organism. The consciousness of being in spiritual health, and anything which confirms this consciousness, is grateful to the pious mind. I take the things I have done "for Christ's sake" as evidence, not that I am personally deserving of his favor, but that the Spirit of Christ, in some measure, is dwelling in me; and this will sometimes start a song, even in the midst of my self-upbraidings. If I am but an earthen vessel, and have often shown my earthly tendencies, I am sure that I am the receptacle of a divine element. If it is but a few sheaves that I can point to as the result of my gleanings in the Master's field, I am sure that it is the power of grace which has prompted and enabled me to gather even these scanty treasures. And I am sure my Lord will not disown kinship with one who bears in his soul even so faint a reflection of his own image. As I see the night in which no man can work darkening around me, I prize the recollection of any poor labors I have performed for Christ as the truest successes of my life; and I do not believe that any Christian, on his death-bed, ever complained that he had done or suffered too much in the service of his Master.

Another reflection which has been a solace

to me is, that there is a potency which we call influence with which every man is charged, and by which, when under the direction of Christian rule and motive, he may be the instrument in effecting indefinite good. I confess I am filled with awe when I open my mind to the thought of this invisible power which is emanating from myself, and from everything in the world around me. I am the author of influence, and the subject of influence, whether I will it or not—whether I know it or not. It is like the fluid which pours itself through the minute veins in the body of a tree, the effect of which appears in the fruit of the olive and the vine, or in the poisonous secretions of the upas tree. I am not much surprised at the grand old illusion of the astrologers, that the planets were concerned in shaping the destiny of men and nations on the earth, for it was but an unscientific application of the truth that influence is present and active everywhere. Their mistake was in locating in the stars a subtle power which really resides in man.

Where the supreme desire is to make life effective in producing ameliorating and beneficent results, what an incalculable encouragement for effort and what a boundless field to operate upon does this idea furnish! We do not see where the impressions we originate touch the lives of those with whom we associate; it is best, perhaps, that we should not; but by a law of the universe they abide and perpetuate themselves, and sweep on over ages and generations. Surely, it is worth while to covet and to cultivate an endowment like this, and to appreciate it as a sacred trust! What do we see in the charitable institutions of to-day but the effect of the widow's "two mites," and the Samaritan's "oil and wine," preserved to us in the Bible, to teach us, among other lessons, perhaps, the potency of personal influence?

I am thankful to be able to believe that in my contracted sphere I have tried to exercise a salutary influence. I persuade myself that in some quarters, as in my home, I have seen the good results of it. And I have been cheered, in several instances, by letters received from persons almost forgotten, giving testimony to the sucess of my humble efforts, in past years, to lead the writers to the love of God and the practice of religion.

And one other conviction is fastened in my mind. I revert with profound gratitude to the good hand of the Lord which was upon me in constraining me to accept the office of ruling elder in the church, against which my inclinatious so strongly rebelled. I have been recompensed a thousand times over for all the anxieties, toils, and mortifications a consent to take up the burden cost me. The assumption of the office has caused me to lean more habitually upon the promised grace of God in my Christian life. It has been a check upon the inordinate claims of worldly business, and a protection to the spiritual side of my nature. It has given me facilities and opportunities for engaging in religious work. It has developed faculties which would otherwise have remained latent or inert. It has been to me, in all respects, an eminent means of grace. It has helped me, by the experience through which it has led me, to gather around me cheering views of God's ways of dealing with me. It has hung around the evening of my life memories and hopes as radiant as those golden cloudlets which I marked at the close of this winter's day, convoying the setting sun to his rest.

Oh, yes, with a full heart "I thank Christ Jesus, my Lord," and I expect to thank him throughout eternity, "that he has counted me worthy to be put into this ministry," and given me ability and fidelity, in some feeble measure, to do him service therein.

And were it in my power, I would leave it

as a dying charge to all to whom a call to labor in this capacity, in the edifying of the church of God, may be addressed, "Fear not; be strong; go up to the mountains and bring wood, and build the house, for I AM WITH YOU, SAITH THE LORD!"

www.ingramcontent.com/pod-product-compliance
Lightning Source LLC
Chambersburg PA
CBHW020306170426
43202CB00008B/512